Hedda Gabler

by Henrik Ibsen

A New Version

by Christopher Hampton

A Samuel French Acting Edition

SAMUELFRENCH.COM

ISBN 978-0-573-61009-7 Printed in U.S.A. #00532

HEDDA GABLER, a new adaptation by Christopher Hampton of the Henrik Ibsen play from a literal translation by Hélène Grégoire, was given its New York presentation at the Playhouse Theatre. The producer was Hillard Elkins and it was directed by Patrick Garland. Sets, Costumes and Lighting were by John Bury. The production supervisor was Michael Thoma with the associate producer George Platt. The cast was as follows:

CAST

(*In Order of Appearance*)

AUNT JULIA .... *Kate Wilkinson*

BERTE .... *Eda Reiss Merin*

GEORGE TESMAN .... *Roy Shuman*

HEDDA GABLER .... *Claire Bloom*

MRS. ELVSTED .... *Patricia Elliott*

JUDGE BRACK .... *Robert Gerringer*

EILERT LOVBORG .... *Donald Madden*

The action takes place in Tesman's villa in the fashionable quarter of town.

ACT ONE

Morning

ACT TWO

Afternoon

INTERMISSION

ACT THREE

The next day at dawn

ACT FOUR

Evening

Hedda Gabler

ACT ONE

A spacious, attractive and tastefully furnished drawing room, decorated in dark colors. At the back, a wide doorway, which leads, as we can see through the open curtains, into a smaller room decorated in the same style as the drawing room. In the right-hand wall of the front room, a double door, which leads out into the hall, is partly visible. In the opposite wall, on the L., *a glass door, also with open curtains. Through this door we can see a covered verandah and trees in autumn colors. In the foreground, an oval table with a cover and a number of chairs. Downstage, on the right-hand wall, a large dark porcelain stove, a high-backed armchair, a footstool with a cushion and two other stools. Upstage, in the right-hand corner, a sofa and small round table. Another sofa* D. L., *a little away from the wall.* U. *of the glass door, a grand piano. Whatnots, with terra cotta and majolica ornaments, on either side of the doorway at the back. Against the back wall of the inner room, a table and a couple of chairs. Above the sofa, the portrait of a handsome, elderly man in a general's uniform. Above the table a hanging lamp with an opaque, milk-white glass shade. Around the drawing room, a number of vases and glasses with flowers in them. More flowers lying on the tables. The floors in both rooms are thickly carpeted.*

Early morning. The sun streams in through the glass door. MISS JULIANA TESMAN, *wearing a hat and carrying her parasol, comes in from the hall, followed by* BERTE, *who carries a bunch of flowers wrapped in paper.* MISS TESMAN *is about 65; she looks pleasant and kindly and is dressed neatly but simply in a gray outdoor suit.* BERTE, *the maid, is getting on in years; she looks plain and somewhat rustic.* MISS TESMAN *stops just inside the door, listens and speaks quietly.*

MISS TESMAN. My goodness, are they still in bed?

BERTE. (*Also quietly.*) That's what I was telling you, miss. You know how late the steamer got in last night. And then there was all that unpacking Mrs. Tesman had to do before she could go to bed, I don't know.

MISS TESMAN. Oh, well, let them have a good sleep. It's a lovely morning for them when they do get up.

BERTE. (*By the table, not knowing where to put the flowers.*) I think I'll just put these over here, miss.

MISS TESMAN. Well, Berte dear, you've got a new master and mistress now. God knows, parting with you was almost more than I could bear.

BERTE. (*Close to tears.*) What do you think it's like for me, miss? It's years and years I've been working for you.

MISS TESMAN. We'll have to make the best of it, Berte. There's nothing else we can do. George depends on you, you see: completely. After all, you have looked after him since he was a little boy.

BERTE. Yes, but I can't stop thinking about Miss Rina, miss. Lying at home there, absolutely helpless, poor thing. And that new maid. She'll never learn how to look after an invalid properly, never.

MISS TESMAN. Oh, it won't take me long to teach her. Anyway, I shall see to most of the work myself. You needn't worry about my poor sister, Berte, dear.

BERTE. But that's not the only thing, miss. I'm so frightened Mrs. Tesman will think I'm not suitable.

MISS TESMAN. Oh, well, there might be one or two things when you first start . . .

BERTE. She does seem a bit superior.

MISS TESMAN. Well, that's only to be expected. She is General Gabler's daughter. Think what sort of a life she must have had when the general was alive. Do you remember how she used to go out riding with her father? That long, black riding outfit? And the feather in her hat?

BERTE. Yes, oh yes, I do. But I never thought then she would finish up marrying our little student.

MISS TESMAN. No, I didn't either. Not that George is a student any more, Berte. From now on, you'll have to call him Dr. Tesman.

BERTE. So Mrs. Tesman was saying last night, soon as they set foot in the house. Is that really true, miss?

MISS TESMAN. Certainly. It's wonderful, isn't it, Berte, he was made a doctor while he was abroad, you know, on his tour. First thing I heard about it was when he told me last night on the quay.

BERTE. Well, I don't know, I'm sure he's clever enough to do anything. But I never thought he'd take up medicine.

MISS TESMAN. No, no, no, he's not that kind of doctor. (*Nods meaningfully.*) You might have to call him something even more important soon.

BERTE. And what might that be, miss?

MISS TESMAN. (*Smiling.*) Aha, wouldn't you like to know? (*Moved.*) Oh, dear, oh dear, if only poor Jochum could come back from the dead and see what's happened to his little boy. (*Looks around.*) Just a minute, Berte, what have you done? Why have you taken the loose covers off the furniture?

BERTE. Mrs. Tesman said. She said she can't stand loose covers on the chairs.

MISS TESMAN. They're not going to use this room for everyday, are they?

BERTE. Yes, I think so. That's what Mrs. Tesman said, anyway. He, er, the doctor, I mean, didn't say anything.

(GEORGE TESMAN *enters through the inner room, hum-*

ming and carrying a small, empty suitcase. He is a young-looking man of average height, about 33, quite plump, with a round, open, cheerful face, and blond hair and beard. He wears glasses and comfortable, somewhat shabby indoor clothes.)

MISS TESMAN. Good morning, George, good morning!

TESMAN. (*In the doorway.*) Auntie Julia! (*Goes over to her and shakes her hand enthusiastically.*) Dear Auntie Julia. All this way. At this hour of the morning, mm?

MISS TESMAN. Well, I wanted to come and see how you were getting on.

TESMAN. But you can't have had a proper night's sleep.

MISS TESMAN. Oh, that doesn't matter at all.

TESMAN. Well. You . . . er . . . got home all right from the quay. Mm?

MISS TESMAN. Yes, quite all right, thank goodness. The judge was kind enough to see me all the way to my door.

TESMAN. We were terribly sorry there wasn't room for you in our carriage. But you could see what a lot of luggage Hedda brought with her, couldn't you?

MISS TESMAN. Yes, she certainly had a great deal of luggage.

BERTE. (*To* TESMAN.) Shall I go and ask Mrs. Tesman if there's anything I can do to help?

TESMAN. No, thank you, Berte, never mind. She said she'd ring if she wanted anything.

BERTE. (*Moving toward the* R.) All right, then.

TESMAN. One thing, look, could you just put this suitcase away somewhere?

BERTE. (*Taking it.*) I'll put it in the attic. (*Goes out through the hall door.*)

TESMAN. Can you imagine, Auntie, that suitcase was absolutely bursting with copies I made of various documents. All those archives I looked at, I made the most incredible discoveries. Strange forgotten details nobody else knows anything about.

MISS TESMAN. Well, you don't seem to have wasted any time on your honeymoon, George.

TESMAN. No, I haven't, no, no. Why don't you take your bonnet off, Auntie? Look. May I undo the bow, mm?

MISS TESMAN. (*As he does so.*) Dear, oh, dear, it's just as if you'd never left home.

TESMAN. (*Turning the hat around in his hand.*) What a lovely smart hat you've bought yourself.

MISS TESMAN. I bought it because of Hedda.

TESMAN. Mm? Because of Hedda?

MISS TESMAN. Yes, so Hedda wouldn't be ashamed of me if we went out for a walk.

TESMAN. (*Stroking her cheek.*) Really, you think of everything, Auntie Julia. (*Puts the hat down on a chair by the table.*) Now. Look. Why don't we sit down on the sofa and have a little chat before Hedda joins us?

(*They sit down. She puts her parasol in a corner on the sofa.*)

MISS TESMAN. (*Taking both his hands and looking at him.*) It's marvelous to see you again, George, sitting there large as life. Poor Jochum's little boy.

TESMAN. And for me, Auntie Julia, to see you. I mean, to me, you've always seemed like a mother and a father.

MISS TESMAN. Yes, I'm sure you'll go on being fond of your old aunt.

TESMAN. And how's Auntie Rina? Is there any improvement, mm?

MISS TESMAN. Oh no, poor thing, I don't think we can hope for any improvement. There she is, lying there just as helpless as she has been all these years. I only hope God lets me keep her for a little bit longer. Otherwise, I wouldn't know what to do with my life, George. Especially now I haven't got you to look after any more.

TESMAN. (*Patting her on the back.*) Now then, there, there.

MISS TESMAN. (*A sudden change of tone.*) I can't get over the fact that you're married now, George. And to Hedda Gabler of all people, the beautiful Hedda Gabler. It's amazing, when you think of how many admirers she used to have.

TESMAN. (*Humming a little and smiling complacently.*) Yes, I should think quite a few of my friends in town must be pretty jealous, don't you think, mm?

MISS TESMAN. And you had such a lovely long honeymoon—five, no more than that, nearly six months.

TESMAN. Well, I did have a lot of research to do. Investigating all those archives, and ploughing through mountains of books.

MISS TESMAN. Yes, I know you did. (*Lowers her voice confidentially.*) Listen, George, you haven't, you haven't anything special to tell me, have you?

TESMAN. About the tour?

MISS TESMAN. Yes.

TESMAN. No, I don't think there was anything except what I told you in my letters. I took my doctor's degree abroad, but I told you about that yesterday.

MISS TESMAN. Yes, yes, I know about that. What I meant was I was wondering if you had any . . . expectations.

TESMAN. Expectations?

MISS TESMAN. Oh, George, I am your auntie after all.

TESMAN. Well, of course I've got expectations.

MISS TESMAN. You have?

TESMAN. Yes, I expect to be made a professor before very long. That's my main expectation.

MISS TESMAN. To be made a professor?

TESMAN. Yes, I might even say it's a certainty. But, Auntie, you know about that already, dear.

MISS TESMAN. (*Chuckling.*) Yes, you're right, I do, yes. (*Changes the subject.*) But your tour must have cost an awful lot of money, George.

TESMAN. Yes, well, the scholarship was very generous, that went quite a long way towards it.

MISS TESMAN. Yes, but what I can't understand is how you stretched it out to pay for both of you.

TESMAN. Ah, that is rather extraordinary, isn't it, mm?

MISS TESMAN. Not only that, but they always say traveling with a lady is inordinately expensive.

TESMAN. Yes, that's to be expected, it does mean a little extra expense. But Hedda had to have that trip, Auntie. Really, she had to. It was the least I could do.

MISS TESMAN. Yes, I suppose so. People always seem to insist on a honeymoon trip nowadays. Now, what I want to know is whether you've had a proper look round the house yet.

TESMAN. Oh, yes, I've been up and about since dawn.

MISS TESMAN. And what do you think of it?

TESMAN. It's marvelous. Absolutely marvelous. The only thing I'm not sure about is what we're going to do with the two empty rooms between the back room there and Hedda's bedroom.

MISS TESMAN. (*Chuckling.*) Ah, George, dear, I expect you'll find some use for them, sooner or later.

TESMAN. Yes, Auntie, I'm sure you're right. Somewhere to put all those extra books I'll have to get, mm?

MISS TESMAN. Yes, dear, books, yes, that's what I meant.

TESMAN. Anyway, it's because of Hedda that I'm really pleased about this. Before we were engaged she always used to say the only place she really wanted to live was Senator Falk's villa.

MISS TESMAN. Amazing that it should have come up for sale just after you went away.

TESMAN. Yes, Auntie, the luck's really been on our side, hasn't it, mm?

MISS TESMAN. But it's expensive, isn't it, George? It's all going to be very expensive.

TESMAN. (*Somewhat crestfallen.*) Yes, I suppose it is.

MISS TESMAN. Of course it is.

TESMAN. How much would you say? I mean approximately? Mm?

MISS TESMAN. Won't be able to tell until the accounts come in.

TESMAN. Well, luckily Judge Brack has managed to get me the very best terms. He wrote to Hedda about it.

MISS TESMAN. There's no need to worry about it, dear. I've given a guarantee for the furniture and all the carpets.

TESMAN. Guarantee? You have? But how could you, Auntie? What kind of guarantee?

MISS TESMAN. I've taken out a mortgage on our annuity.

TESMAN. (*Jumping to his feet.*) What? You mean on the annuity you and Auntie Rina . . .

MISS TESMAN. Well, I couldn't think what else to do.

TESMAN. (*Standing in front of her.*) But, Auntie, have you gone mad? Mm? Your annuity is the only thing you and Auntie Rina have to live on.

MISS TESMAN. Now, don't upset yourself. It's only a formality, you know. That's what Judge Brack said. He was kind enough to make all the arrangements for me. And he said it was only a formality.

TESMAN. Yes, that's as may be. All the same . . .

MISS TESMAN. Anyway, from now on you'll have your salary coming in. And, good Lord, what if it does cost us a bit? A little something to start you off with, you know we'd be only too pleased.

TESMAN. Oh, Auntie, you're always ready to make sacrifices for me.

MISS TESMAN. (*Getting up and putting her hand on his shoulder.*) My dear boy, what other pleasures do I have in this world, besides helping to smooth your way? After all, you've had no father or mother to turn to. And we've got what we were aiming for now. Sometimes things have seemed very black. But, thank God, George, you've come through it all.

TESMAN. Yes, strange, isn't it, how everything has worked out for the best?

MISS TESMAN. Yes, and the people who were against you and wanted to hold you back have come to grief, George, and fallen by the wayside. The most dangerous of them all was the one that fell the hardest. And as he made his bed, so he must lie on it, poor misguided wretch.

TESMAN. Erm, have you had any more news about Eilert? Since I went away, I mean.

MISS TESMAN. No. Except he's supposed to have published some new book.

TESMAN. Really? What, Eilert Lovborg? Recent, is that, mm?

MISS TESMAN. Yes, apparently. Goodness knows whether it's any good. Now when *your* new book comes out, George, that'll be a different matter. What's it about?

TESMAN. It's going to be about medieval husbandry in Brabant.

MISS TESMAN. Fancy you being able to write about that sort of thing!

TESMAN. Well, it'll probably be some time before it comes out. I've got all those papers to sort through and catalogue first, you see.

MISS TESMAN. Yes, sorting and cataloguing, you know all about that. You're Jochum's son, all right.

TESMAN. Anyway, I'm certainly looking forward to getting down to work. Especially now I've got my own home sweet home to work in.

MISS TESMAN. And now you've got the wife you set your heart on, George dear, that's the most important thing of all.

TESMAN. (*Putting his arms round her.*) Oh, yes, Auntie, yes. Hedda. She's the most wonderful thing that ever happened to me. (*Looks over to the doorway.*) That's her now, isn't it, mm?

(HEDDA *enters from the* L. *through the back room. She is a woman of 29. Her face and figure are refined and distinguished. Her complexion is pale and lustreless. Her eyes are steel-gray, cold, clear and calm. Her medium brown hair is beautiful, without being particularly abundant. She wears a tasteful, loose-fitting morning gown.*)

MISS TESMAN. (*Going to meet* HEDDA.) Good morning, Hedda, my dear. How are you, good morning.

HEDDA. Good morning, Miss Tesman. How kind of you to call so early.

MISS TESMAN. (*Somewhat embarrassed.*) Well, and . . . er . . . did the bride sleep well in her new home?

HEDDA. Yes, thanks. Reasonably.

TESMAN. (*Laughing.*) Reasonably? Come on, Hedda, you were sleeping like a log when I got up.

HEDDA. Fortunately. It always takes time to get used to anything new, Miss Tesman. It's a gradual business. (*Looks over to the* L.) Tut, the maid's left the verandah door open, all that sun pouring in.

MISS TESMAN. (*Moving toward the door.*) Well, let's shut it, then.

HEDDA. No, no, don't. We could do with some fresh air. All these wretched flowers. Now, won't you sit down, Miss Tesman?

MISS TESMAN. No, thank you. Now I know everything's all right here, I'd better be getting along home. My sister will be lying waiting, she misses me very badly when I'm away.

TESMAN. Don't forget to give her my love. And tell her I'll be popping in to see her later on in the day.

MISS TESMAN. Yes, all right, I will. Oh, by the way, George . . . (*Fumbles in the pocket of her dress.*) I almost forgot, I've got something for you.

TESMAN. What? What is it, Auntie? Mm?

MISS TESMAN. (*Pulling out a flat parcel wrapped in newspaper and handing it to him.*) Here you are, dear.

TESMAN. (*Opening it.*) Oh, Auntie Julia, no, did you

save them for me? Hedda! Isn't that really touching, don't you think, mm?

HEDDA. (*Beside the whatnot on the* R.) Yes, dear. What is it?

TESMAN. My old house shoes. You know, my slippers.

HEDDA. Oh, yes, I remember you talked about them frequently while we were abroad.

TESMAN. Well, I missed them so much. (*Goes over to her.*) Here they are, Hedda, have a look.

HEDDA. (*Crossing to the oven.*) No, thanks, I'd really rather not.

TESMAN. (*Following her.*) Can you imagine, Auntie Rina embroidered them for me herself, even though she was ill in bed. You can't think how many memories they bring back.

HEDDA. (*By the table.*) Not to me.

MISS TESMAN. Hedda has a point there, George.

TESMAN. Yes, but I mean, now she's one of the family . . .

HEDDA. (*Interrupting.*) We'll never be able to put up with that maid, Tesman.

MISS TESMAN. With Berte?

TESMAN. Whatever makes you think that, dear? Mm?

HEDDA. (*Pointing.*) Well, she's left her old hat on the chair, look.

TESMAN. (*Dropping his slippers on the floor in amazement.*) But, Hedda . . .

HEDDA. Anyone could come in and see it.

TESMAN. But, Hedda, that's Auntie Julia's bonnet.

HEDDA. Oh, really?

MISS TESMAN. (*Picking up the hat.*) Yes, it is mine. And it's not old either, Hedda.

HEDDA. I really didn't look at it very carefully, Miss Tesman.

MISS TESMAN. (*Tying the hat on.*) It's actually the first time I've ever worn it, I can assure you of that.

TESMAN. Well, and very nice it is too. Beautiful.

MISS TESMAN. No, George, it's very ordinary. (*Looks*

around her.) Now, where's that parasol? Ah. (*Picks it up.*) That's mine as well. (*Mumbles.*) Not Berte's.

TESMAN. A new hat and a new parasol, can you imagine, Hedda?

HEDDA. Yes, very pretty, lovely.

TESMAN. Yes, they are, aren't they? Mm? Auntie, before you go, have a good look at Hedda. Now she really *is* very pretty and lovely.

MISS TESMAN. Well, my dear, there's nothing surprising about that. Hedda's been beautiful all her life. (*Nods and moves toward the* R.)

TESMAN. (*Following.*) Yes, but have you noticed how chubby and healthy she looks? She really filled out while we were abroad.

HEDDA. (*Crossing the room.*) Oh, that's enough!

MISS TESMAN. (*Stops and turns round.*) Filled out?

TESMAN. Yes, Auntie, it doesn't show very much when she's got that dress on. But I'm lucky enough . . .

HEDDA. (*By the glass door, impatiently.*) You're not lucky enough for anything.

TESMAN. It's probably the mountain air in the Tyrol . . .

HEDDA. (*Interrupting curtly.*) I'm exactly the same now as I was when I went away.

TESMAN. So you keep saying. But you're not. Don't you agree with me, Auntie?

MISS TESMAN. (*Stands looking at her with folded hands.*) Hedda is beautiful, beautiful, beautiful. (*Goes up to her, takes her head in both hands, bends it forward and kisses her hair.*) God bless you and keep you, Hedda Tesman. For George's sake.

HEDDA. (*Gently freeing herself.*) Oh . . . let go of me.

MISS TESMAN. (*Quietly moved.*) I shall come and see you both every day.

TESMAN. Yes, Auntie, you make sure you do, mm?

MISS TESMAN. Good-bye. Good-bye.

(*She goes out through the hall door.* TESMAN *follows her, leaving the door ajar. We hear* TESMAN *repeating his good wishes to Auntie Rina and his thanks for the slippers. Meanwhile,* HEDDA *walks across the room and raises her arms, clenching her hands as if in anger. She draws the curtains in front of the glass door and stands there looking out. A moment later,* TESMAN *reappears, closing the door behind him.*)

TESMAN. (*Picking up his slippers from the floor.*) What are you up to, Hedda?

HEDDA. (*Calm and controlled now.*) I'm just standing here looking at the leaves. They're so yellow. And dried up.

TESMAN. (*Wrapping up the slippers and putting them down on the table.*) Yes, well, we are well into September now, after all.

HEDDA. (*Restless again.*) Yes, we are. Already in . . . into September.

TESMAN. Didn't you think Auntie Julia was a bit odd today? Sort of formal? Any idea what was the matter with her? Mm?

HEDDA. I hardly know her. Isn't she usually like that?

TESMAN. No, not as a rule.

HEDDA. (*Moving away from the glass door.*) Was she upset by what I said about her hat, do you think?

TESMAN. Oh, not particularly. Perhaps at the time she was a little.

HEDDA. But fancy leaving your hat lying around like that in the drawing room. It's just not done, that sort of thing.

TESMAN. Well, I'm sure Auntie Julia won't do it again.

HEDDA. Anyway, I shall try to make it up with her.

TESMAN. Yes, Hedda, if you could, dear, that would be nice.

HEDDA. When you go and see them this afternoon, why don't you ask her over this evening?

TESMAN. Yes, I will, I will. And there's one other thing you could do that would really make her happy.

HEDDA. What?

TESMAN. If you could perhaps stop calling her Miss Tesman, mm? For my sake.

HEDDA. No, Tesman, I couldn't. You mustn't keep asking me, we've discussed this before. If you like I'll try to call her Aunt, all right? But that's the best I can do.

TESMAN. It's just that now you're one of the family . . .

HEDDA. I can't see what . . . (*Crosses over to the door.*)

TESMAN. (*After a pause.*) Is anything the matter? Mm?

HEDDA. I'm just looking at my old piano. It doesn't go very well with all the other things.

TESMAN. Well, as soon as I start getting my salary, we'll see about getting it exchanged.

HEDDA. Exchanged? That's not what I meant, I don't want to get rid of it. I thought we could move it into the back room there, and get another one to put here in its place. I mean, as soon as we can manage it.

TESMAN. (*Slightly dejected.*) Oh. Yes, well, why not?

HEDDA. (*Picking the bouquet up from the piano.*) These flowers weren't here when we got in last night.

TESMAN. Auntie Julia probably brought them for you.

HEDDA. (*Examining the bouquet.*) Here's a visiting card. (*Takes it out and reads it.*) "Will call in again later on today." Guess who it's from.

TESMAN. I don't know. Who? Mm?

HEDDA. It says "Mrs. Elvsted."

TESMAN. Really? Wasn't she Miss Rysing? Before she married Sheriff Elvsted?

HEDDA. Yes, that's right. She had that irritating hair she was always flaunting. I was told she was an old flame of yours.

TESMAN. (*Laughing.*) Oh, not for very long. And that

was before I met you, Hedda. But what's she doing in town? It's extraordinary.

HEDDA. It's strange she should want to call on us. I haven't seen her since I left school.

TESMAN. Yes, it's God knows how long since I saw her. I don't know how she puts up with it, living up there in that out-of-the-way hole, do you? Mm?

HEDDA. (*Considers a moment and then says suddenly.*) Listen, Tesman, isn't he . . . doesn't Eilert Lovborg live somewhere up round there?

TESMAN. Yes, somewhere in that area.

(BERTE *appears in the hall doorway.*)

BERTE. That lady who called a while ago and left some flowers is here again, madam. (*Points to the flowers.*) Those flowers you're holding.

HEDDA. Oh, is she? Would you show her in, please? (BERTE *opens the door for* MRS. ELVSTED *and goes out herself.* MRS. ELVSTED *is a fragile-looking woman with beautiful, soft features. Her eyes are pale blue, large, round and somewhat protruding, with a frightened and puzzled expression. Her hair is remarkably fair, almost flaxen, abundant and wavy. She is a few years younger than* HEDDA. *She wears a dark morning suit, tasteful, but not quite in the latest fashion. Approaching her warmly.*) How are you, Mrs. Elvsted? It's lovely to see you again.

MRS. ELVSTED. (*Trying to control her nervousness.*) Well, it's been a very long time . . .

TESMAN. (*Stretching out his hand.*) Yes, it has, hasn't it? Mm?

HEDDA. Thank you for the beautiful flowers.

MRS. ELVSTED. Oh, that's all right. . . . I wanted to come straight here yesterday afternoon, but I heard you were still away. . . .

TESMAN. You've just arrived in town, have you? Mm?

MRS. ELVSTED. Yesterday afternoon. I got quite desperate when I found out you weren't at home.

HEDDA. Desperate? Why?

TESMAN. But, my dear Mrs. Rysing . . . I mean, Mrs. Elvsted.

HEDDA. I hope there's nothing wrong.

MRS. ELVSTED. Yes, there is. And I don't know a single person here I can turn to, except for you.

HEDDA. (*Putting the bouquet down on the table.*) Come on, let's sit down here on the sofa.

MRS. ELVSTED. Oh, no, I feel much too restless to sit down.

HEDDA. Of course you don't. Come on. (*Pushes* MRS. ELVSTED *down on the sofa and sits next to her.*)

TESMAN. Now, what's the matter, Mrs. erm . . . ?

HEDDA. Is there something wrong at home?

MRS. ELVSTED. Yes, well, there is and there isn't. The thing is, I don't want you to misunderstand me.

HEDDA. Well then, you'd better tell us everything as plainly as possible.

TESMAN. After all, I expect that's why you came, isn't it, mm?

MRS. ELVSTED. Yes, of course it is . . . well . . . I should tell you, if you don't already know, that Eilert Lovborg is here in town somewhere.

HEDDA. Lovborg . . .

TESMAN. No, really, has Eilert Lovborg come back? Did you hear that, Hedda? Extraordinary!

HEDDA. Of course I heard, my God.

MRS. ELVSTED. He's been here about a week already. A whole week. Alone. In this dangerous town, just think. Mixing in all that bad company.

HEDDA. But, my dear Mrs. Elvsted, what's he got to do with you?

MRS. ELVSTED. (*Frightened, she looks up at* HEDDA *and speaks quickly.*) Oh, well, he was the . . . er . . . children's tutor.

HEDDA. You have children?

MRS. ELVSTED. No, no, I don't. They're my husband's.

HEDDA. Oh, your stepchildren.

MRS. ELVSTED. Yes.

TESMAN. (*Groping for the words.*) But was he sufficiently . . . er . . . I don't quite know how to put this . . . was he um sufficiently regular in his way of life to be suitable for a job like that? Mm?

MRS. ELVSTED. In the last two years his behavior has been impeccable.

TESMAN. Has it? Really? Extraordinary. Did you hear that, Hedda?

HEDDA. Yes, I did.

MRS. ELVSTED. Impeccable. I promise you. In every way. But even so, now I know he's here, in a big town, with all that money on him . . . I'm terrified of what might happen to him.

TESMAN. But why didn't he stay where he was? With you and your husband? Mm?

MRS. ELVSTED. Since his book was published, he hasn't really been able to settle down at home.

TESMAN. Yes, that's right. Auntie Julia told me he'd published a new book.

MRS. ELVSTED. Yes, it's a wonderful new book about the processes of civilization, sort of a general outline. It's been out about a fortnight. It's sold very well, a lot of people have read it, it's caused something of a sensation . . .

TESMAN. Has it? I suppose it must be something he's been saving since . . . happier days.

MRS. ELVSTED. Do you mean some time ago?

TESMAN. Yes.

MRS. ELVSTED. Oh, no, he's written it all since he came to us . . . over the last year.

TESMAN. Well, that's good tidings, isn't it, Hedda? Extraordinary.

MRS. ELVSTED. Yes, if only it would last.

HEDDA. Have you found him yet?

MRS. ELVSTED. No, not yet. I had the greatest difficulty tracking down his address. But I finally managed to this morning.

HEDDA. (*Looking inquiringly at her.*) Actually, I think it's a bit strange that your husband . . . ah . . .

MRS. ELVSTED. (*Starting nervously.*) My husband? What do you mean?

HEDDA. Well, that he should send you into town to run his errands. And not come in himself to look after his friend.

MRS. ELVSTED. Oh, no, my husband's got no time for that kind of thing. Anyway, I had some shopping to do.

HEDDA. (*Ghost of a smile.*) Oh, well, then . . .

MRS. ELVSTED. (*Getting up hastily and rather uneasily.*) I just wanted to ask you, Mr. Tesman, please be kind to Eilert Lovborg if he comes to see you, please. Because I'm sure he will. After all, you used to be very close friends. And aren't you both studying the same subject? You're in the same faculty, aren't you? As far as I can remember.

TESMAN. Used to be, anyway, yes.

MRS. ELVSTED. Well then, please, can I ask you very seriously to keep a sharp eye on him, as well? Will you promise me that, Mr. Tesman, will you?

TESMAN. Of course, it'll be a pleasure, Mrs. Rysing. . . .

HEDDA. Elvsted.

TESMAN. I'll do anything I can for Eilert, I promise. You can rely on me.

MRS. ELVSTED. That's terribly kind of you. (*Presses his hands.*) Thank you, thank you, thank you. (*Frightened.*) It's my husband, you see, he thinks such a lot of him.

HEDDA. (*Getting up.*) You ought to write to him, Tesman. Otherwise he might hesitate about coming round to see you.

TESMAN. Yes, Hedda, perhaps that might be the best way of going about things, do you think? Mm?

HEDDA. The sooner the better. Now, I'd say.

MRS. ELVSTED. (*Imploringly.*) Oh, why don't you?

TESMAN. I'll write to him now, Mrs. erm, this minute. Have you got his address, Mrs. . . . Elvsted?

MRS. ELVSTED. Yes. (*Takes a small piece of paper out of her pocket and gives it to him.*) Here.

TESMAN. Good, well done. I'll go and do it now then. (*Casts about him.*) Just a minute. Where are my slippers? Oh, yes. (*Picks up the packet and is on his way out.*)

HEDDA. Make it a warm, friendly letter, will you? And long.

TESMAN. Right.

MRS. ELVSTED. But don't tell him I asked you, please, will you?

TESMAN. Of course not, that goes without saying, doesn't it? Mm? (*Exits through the back room.*)

HEDDA. (*Going over to* MRS. ELVSTED, *smiling and speaking in a low voice.*) *That* is killing two birds with one stone.

MRS. ELVSTED. What do you mean?

HEDDA. Couldn't you tell I was trying to get rid of him?

MRS. ELVSTED. Well, yes, to write the letter . . .

HEDDA. And because I wanted to talk to you alone.

MRS. ELVSTED. (*Confused.*) About the same thing?

HEDDA. Exactly.

MRS. ELVSTED. (*Apprehensively.*) But there's nothing more to say about it, Mrs. Tesman. Honestly, nothing.

HEDDA. Oh, yes, there is. A lot. I can tell. Come here. Come and sit down, and we can have a nice, private conversation. (*Forces* MRS. ELVSTED *to sit in the armchair by the stove and then sits on one of the stools.*)

MRS. ELVSTED. (*Looking nervously at her watch.*) But, Mrs. Tesman, I really think it's time I was on my way.

HEDDA. I'm sure you can't be in that much of a hurry. Now. Tell me something about what sort of life you lead at home.

MRS. ELVSTED. That's the last thing I want to talk about.

HEDDA. Even to me? After all, dear, we were at school together.

MRS. ELVSTED. Yes, but you were in the class above me. And I was terribly frightened of you in those days.

HEDDA. Frightened? Of me?

MRS. ELVSTED. Yes. Terribly frightened. When we passed on the stairs you always used to pull my hair.

HEDDA. I didn't, did I?

MRS. ELVSTED. Yes, and one day you said you wanted to set fire to it.

HEDDA. Yes, but that was just fooling about, you must know that.

MRS. ELVSTED. Yes, but I was so stupid in those days. And since then, I mean since we left school, we seem to have drifted such a long . . . such a long way away from each other. We've moved in completely different circles.

HEDDA. Well, now's our chance to get together again. Listen, we used to be very friendly at school. We used to call each other by our Christian names.

MRS. ELVSTED. I don't think so. I think you must be mistaken.

HEDDA. Of course I'm not. No, I remember distinctly. So let's be friends now, as we were in the old days. (*Moves the stool nearer to* MRS. ELVSTED.) All right? (*Kisses her on the cheek.*) And you must call me Hedda.

MRS. ELVSTED. (*Pressing and stroking her hands.*) You're very kind to me. I'm not really used to kindness.

HEDDA. It's all right. I'll be your friend again, as I was before, and call you Thora.

MRS. ELVSTED. Thea it is, actually.

HEDDA. Thea, yes, that's right. Of course. That's what I meant. (*Looks at her sympathetically.*) So, Thea, you're not really used to kindness? Not even in your own home?

MRS. ELVSTED. Well, perhaps if I had a home. But I haven't. I never have had.

HEDDA. (*Considers her for a moment.*) I thought it might be something like that.

MRS. ELVSTED. (*Looking helplessly in front of her.*) Yes . . . yes . . . yes.

HEDDA. I can't quite remember. But when you first went up to the sheriff's house, didn't you go as housekeeper?

MRS. ELVSTED. No, governess they took me on as in the first place. But his wife, I mean his first wife, wasn't very well. She was bedridden most of the time. So I had to look after the house as well.

HEDDA. Until in the end it was your house.

MRS. ELVSTED. (*Sadly.*) Yes, that's right.

HEDDA. Now, let me think. How long is it since you . . . ?

MRS. ELVSTED. Since I got married?

HEDDA. Yes.

MRS. ELVSTED. Five years.

HEDDA. Yes, that's right, it must be.

MRS. ELVSTED. Those five years! Especially the last two or three of them. You can't imagine what it's been like, Mrs. Tesman.

HEDDA. (*Tapping her lightly on the hand.*) Mrs. Tesman? Now really, Thea.

MRS. ELVSTED. Yes, I'm sorry. I'll try . . . Hedda. You can't begin to imagine what it's been like . . .

HEDDA. (*Casually.*) Eilert Lovborg's been up with you for about three years, hasn't he?

MRS. ELVSTED. (*Looking at her dubiously.*) Eilert Lovborg? Yes.

HEDDA. Did you know him before, when you were living here?

MRS. ELVSTED. Not really. I mean, I'd heard of him, obviously.

HEDDA. But when he moved to the country you saw quite a lot of him?

MRS. ELVSTED. Yes, he used to come every day. To give the children lessons. In the end I found I couldn't manage everything on my own.

HEDDA. No, I can understand that. What about your husband? Does he have to do a lot of traveling?

MRS. ELVSTED. Yes. Being sheriff, he has to travel about quite a bit in his district, well, I'm sure you know that, Mrs. . . . er, Hedda.

HEDDA. (*Leaning against the arm of the chair.*) Poor Thea.—Listen, Thea, dear, you're going to tell me everything now, the whole situation.

MRS. ELVSTED. It's better if you ask the questions.

HEDDA. What kind of man is your husband, Thea? I mean, you know, what's he like at home? Is he good to you?

MRS. ELVSTED. (*Evasively.*) Well, I think he believes that everything he does is for the best.

HEDDA. It's just I was thinking he's probably rather old for you. More than twenty years older, isn't he?

MRS. ELVSTED. (*Irritably.*) Yes, there's that as well. And there are other things. Everything about him disgusts me! I mean, we have nothing in common, neither of us, not a single thought.

HEDDA. But he's fond of you, isn't he? In his own way?

MRS. ELVSTED. Oh, I don't know what he is. I'm useful to him anyway, and that's probably as far as it goes. And I don't cost him very much, either. I'm very cheap.

HEDDA. That's very silly of you.

MRS. ELVSTED. (*Shaking her head.*) I've got no choice. Not with him. I don't think he's interested in anyone but himself. Except the children, perhaps.

HEDDA. And Eilert Lovborg.

MRS. ELVSTED. (*Looking at her.*) Eilert Lovborg? What makes you think that?

HEDDA. Well, if he sends you all this way into town to look for him. (*An almost imperceptible smile.*) Anyway, I thought that was what you said to Tesman.

MRS. ELVSTED. (*A nervous twitch.*) Was it? Yes, I suppose it was. (*Quietly, but vehemently.*) I might just as well tell you everything. It's bound to come out sooner or later anyway.

HEDDA. What is, Thea?

MRS. ELVSTED. Well, to cut a long story short, my husband didn't know I was coming.

HEDDA. What? Didn't he know anything about it?

MRS. ELVSTED. Of course he didn't. He wasn't even at home. He's away, traveling. I just couldn't stand it any longer, Hedda! I really couldn't. Spending the rest of my life up there completely on my own.

HEDDA. So . . . ?

MRS. ELVSTED. So I packed a few of my things. What I needed most. As discreetly as I could. And left the house.

HEDDA. Without telling anyone?

MRS. ELVSTED. Yes, and I caught the train into town.

HEDDA. But, Thea, my dear, I don't know how you dared.

MRS. ELVSTED. (*Getting up and crossing the room.*) What else could I have done?

HEDDA. But what's your husband going to say when you get back?

MRS. ELVSTED. (*By the table, looking across at her.*) Back to him?

HEDDA. Well, yes.

MRS. ELVSTED. I'm not going back to him. Ever.

HEDDA. (*Getting up and moving toward her.*) You mean . . . you've left home now . . . for good?

MRS. ELVSTED. Yes. There didn't seem to be any alternative.

HEDDA. What, openly? Just like that?

MRS. ELVSTED. Well, you can't very well keep a thing like that secret, can you?

HEDDA. But, Thea, what do you think people are going to say about all this?

MRS. ELVSTED. I don't know, they can say what they like. (*Sits down sadly and wearily on the sofa.*) What I've done, I did because I had to.

HEDDA. (*After a short silence.*) And what are you thinking of doing now? What's your next move?

MRS. ELVSTED. I don't know. All I know is, that if I'm going to live at all, I must live here, where Eilert Lovborg is.

HEDDA. (*Moving a chair from the table, sitting next to her and stroking her hands.*) Thea, tell me, how did this . . . friendship develop between you and Eilert Lovborg?

MRS. ELVSTED. Oh, it happened gradually. And after a bit I found I had a kind of power over him.

HEDDA. Oh, really?

MRS. ELVSTED. And he started giving up his old habits. Not that I asked him to, I'd never have dared to do that. But I'm sure he noticed how much they upset me. So he just abandoned them.

HEDDA. (*Concealing an involuntary smile of contempt.*) So, little Thea to the rescue, you might say.

MRS. ELVSTED. Well, that's what he says, anyway. And in return he . . . showed me how to be a real human being. Taught me how to think, and how to understand all sorts of things.

HEDDA. So he gave *you* lessons as well, did he?

MRS. ELVSTED. Well, not exactly lessons. He just talked to me. We talked endlessly about everything. And then there was a wonderfully happy time when he let me share in his work. And help him.

HEDDA. He let you do that?

MRS. ELVSTED. Oh, yes! Whenever he wrote anything, we always worked at it together.

HEDDA. Soulmates, were you?

MRS. ELVSTED. (*Enthusiastically.*) Soulmates! It's funny, Hedda, that's what he used to say. I ought to feel gloriously happy. But I can't, because I don't know how long it's going to last.

HEDDA. Don't you trust him any more than that?

MRS. ELVSTED. (*Sadly.*) There's still something between Eilert Lovborg and me. The shadow of a woman.

HEDDA. (*Looking at her in suspense.*) Who?

MRS. ELVSTED. I don't know. Someone in his . . . in the past. Someone he's never quite been able to forget.

HEDDA. What has he hold you about her?

MRS. ELVSTED. He's only ever made one casual reference to her.

HEDDA. And what did he say?

MRS. ELVSTED. He said that when they had to part, she threatened to shoot him with her pistol.

HEDDA. (*Cold, composed.*) Oh, nonsense, people never behave like that.

MRS. ELVSTED. No, that's why I think it must be that red-headed singer he used to . . .

HEDDA. Yes, very probably.

MRS. ELVSTED. I remember hearing about her, apparently she used to carry loaded guns.

HEDDA. Oh, well then, it must have been her.

MRS. ELVSTED. (*Wringing her hands.*) Yes, but the thing is, Hedda, I've just heard that that singer is here in town. Oh, I feel so desperate . . .

HEDDA. (*Glancing toward the back room.*) Sh! Here's Tesman. (*Gets up and whispers.*) Thea, all this is between you and me.

MRS. ELVSTED. (*Jumping up.*) Oh, yes, please, for God's sake . . .

(GEORGE TESMAN *comes in from the* R., *through the back room, holding a letter.*)

TESMAN. Well, there's my missive. All signed and sealed.

HEDDA. Good. I think Mrs. Elvsted has to be going now. Wait a minute. I'll just see her to the garden gate.

TESMAN. Hedda, perhaps Berte could take care of this, could she?

HEDDA. (*Taking the letter.*) Yes, I'll tell her.

(BERTE *comes into the front room.*)

BERTE. Judge Brack is here. He says he'd like to see you.

HEDDA. Yes, show him in, would you? And listen, could you put this letter in the post?

BERTE. (*Taking the letter.*) Yes, madam. (*Opens the door for* JUDGE BRACK, *and then goes out.*)

(*The judge is a man of about 45—thickset, but well-built and supple in his movements. A roundish face with a distinguished profile. His hair is cut short, still almost black, and meticulously groomed. His eyes are lively and alert. His eyebrows are luxuriant, as is his moustache, with the ends clipped short. He wears an elegant walking suit, which is a little too young for him. He uses a monocle, which now and then he lets drop.*)

BRACK. (*Hat in hand, bowing.*) Is it all right to call round so early in the day?

HEDDA. Of course it's all right.

TESMAN. (*Shaking his hand.*) You're always welcome. (*Introducing him.*) Judge Brack, Miss Rysing . . .

HEDDA. Oh . . .

BRACK. (*Bowing.*) Pleased to meet you.

HEDDA. (*Looking at him and smiling.*) I'm not used to seeing you in daylight, Judge.

BRACK. Do I look different?

HEDDA. A little younger, I think.

BRACK. Thank you kindly.

TESMAN. And what about Hedda, mm? Isn't she looking well? She's actually . . .

HEDDA. Oh, don't keep on about me. You'd do better to thank Judge Brack for all the trouble he's taken.

BRACK. But that was my pleasure.

HEDDA. You're very devoted. Look, my friend here's wanting to get away. I'll see you in a minute, Judge. I won't be long.

(*General salutations.* MRS. ELVSTED *and* HEDDA *go out through the hall door.*)

BRACK. Well, is your wife reasonably pleased?

TESMAN. Yes, we can't thank you enough. I mean, she tells me there are still one or two changes she wants made. And a few things she still needs. So I expect we shall have to make a few more minor purchases.

BRACK. Oh? Really?

TESMAN. But we're not going to bother you any more. . . . Hedda said that what she needed she would see to herself. Let's sit down, shall we, mm?

BRACK. Yes, all right, thank you, just for a minute. (*Sits down by the table.*) There's something I wanted to talk to you about, Tesman.

TESMAN. Is there? Oh, I know. (*Sits down.*) I suppose it's time for the after-dinner speeches now, is it, fundamentals, mm?

BRACK. You mean the financial arrangements, oh no, there's nothing very pressing about them. Although I'm beginning to wish we'd set about things a little more modestly.

TESMAN. But how could we have done? What about Hedda? You know her well enough by now, don't you? You know I couldn't possibly expect her to put up with a life of genteel poverty.

BRACK. No, well, that's just the problem, isn't it?

TESMAN. Anyway, fortunately it won't be very long now before I'm given my appointment.

BRACK. Well, that sort of thing is quite often a lengthy process.

TESMAN. You haven't heard anything more about it, have you? Mm?

BRACK. No, nothing definite. . . . (*Breaks off.*) There is one thing. I do have one piece of news for you.

TESMAN. What?

BRACK. Your old friend, Eilert Lovborg, has arrived in town.

TESMAN. Yes, I know.

BRACK. Oh? How did you find that out?

TESMAN. That friend of Hedda's told us.

BRACK. Oh. What was her name? I didn't catch it.

TESMAN. Mrs. Elvsted.

BRACK. Oh, the sheriff's wife. Yes, he's been living up round there somewhere, hasn't he?

TESMAN. Yes, and I was delighted to hear that he'd turned over a new leaf.

BRACK. Apparently.

TESMAN. Extraordinary. And I gather he's published a new book, hasn't he? Mm?

BRACK. He has, yes.

TESMAN. And it seems to have created something of a sensation.

BRACK. Quite an unusual sensation.

TESMAN. Extraordinary. That's very good news, isn't it? He's exceptionally talented. I was terribly afraid he would go completely to pieces.

BRACK. That's what everybody thought.

TESMAN. But what's he going to do now? How's he going to make a living? Mm?

(*As* TESMAN *is finishing his sentence,* HEDDA *enters through the hall door.*)

HEDDA. (*To* BRACK, *laughing with a certain contempt.*) Tesman's always worrying about how people are going to make a living.

TESMAN. We're just talking about poor Eilert Lovborg, dear.

HEDDA. (*Looking sharply at him.*) Oh? (*Sits down in the armchair by the fire and asks casually.*) What's the matter with him?

TESMAN. Well, he frittered away his inheritance a long time ago. And he can hardly get a new book out every year, can he? Mm? So I was wondering what was going to become of him.

BRACK. I might be able to give you some information about that.

TESMAN. Oh?

BRACK. You must remember his relatives have quite a lot of influence.

TESMAN. Yes, but unfortunately his relatives have completely washed their hands of him.

BRACK. At one time he was thought of as the white hope of the family.

TESMAN. Yes, yes, at one time. But he ruined all that himself.

HEDDA. Who knows? (*A thin smile.*) While he was at Sheriff Elvsted's, they're supposed to have rescued him.

BRACK. And then there's this book he's published.

TESMAN. Yes, well, I hope to God they can help him find something to do. I've just written to him. I invited him to come and see us this evening, Hedda.

BRACK. But, Tesman, I thought you were coming to my bachelor party this evening. You promised last night, on the quay.

HEDDA. Had you forgotten, Tesman?

TESMAN. Yes. Completely.

BRACK. Anyway, I'm sure he won't come.

TESMAN. What makes you think that? Mm?

BRACK. (*Hesitating, gets up and puts his hands on the back of the chair.*) My dear Tesman, and you too, Mrs. Tesman, there's something I think it wouldn't be fair not to tell you about, it's . . . it's . . .

TESMAN. About Eilert?

BRACK. About you and him.

TESMAN. Well then, you'd better tell us.

BRACK. You ought to be prepared for your appointment not to be quite as automatic as you hope and expect.

TESMAN. (*Jumping up uneasily.*) Why, has it been blocked in some way? Mm?

BRACK. It's possible that the award of the post may depend on the results of a competition.

TESMAN. A competition! What about that, Hedda, extraordinary!

HEDDA. (*Leaning further back in her chair.*) So that's it. . . .

TESMAN. But against whom? Surely not . . .

BRACK. Precisely. Eilert Lovborg.

TESMAN. (*Wringing his hands.*) But this is quite incredible! It's quite impossible! Isn't it? Mm?

BRACK. All the same, I think that's what's going to happen.

TESMAN. But, I mean, after all, Judge Brack, that would be unbelievably inconsiderate. (*Waves his arms about.*) I mean, I am a married man. And we married because we were counting on that, Hedda and I. Ran up all those debts. And borrowed money from Auntie Julia as well. My God, I'd more or less been promised that job, hadn't I? Mm?

BRACK. Now, calm down, I'm sure you'll get it in the end. After this contest.

HEDDA. (*Motionless in the armchair.*) It's rather exciting, isn't it, Tesman? Like a race.

TESMAN. Oh, Hedda, my dear, I don't see how you can be so casual about it.

HEDDA. (*As before.*) But I'm not. I'm really quite anxious to see what happens.

BRACK. In any case, Mrs. Tesman, I think it's quite a good thing you should know what the situation is. Before you start making those little purchases I gather you're threatening.

HEDDA. I don't see what difference this can make.

BRACK. Don't you? Well, that's up to you. Good-bye. (*To* TESMAN.) When I take my afternoon walk, I'll call by to collect you.

TESMAN. Yes, do. I don't know what to think about this.

HEDDA. (*Lying down and stretching out a hand.*) Good-bye, Judge, come back soon.

BRACK. I will. Good-bye, good-bye.

TESMAN. (*Accompanying him to the door.*) Good-bye, Judge, I'm sorry about all this. (JUDGE BRACK *exits by the hall door. Crossing the room.*) You see, Hedda, that's what comes of setting off on these wild adventures, isn't it? Mm?

HEDDA. (*Looks at him, smiling.*) Experienced at that, are you?

TESMAN. Well, you must admit it was rather adventurous to marry and set up home on nothing but expectations.

HEDDA. You may be right.

TESMAN. Well, anyway, Hedda, we have our beautiful home. Isn't that true? Our dream house. The house we fell in love with, you might almost say, don't you think, mm?

HEDDA. (*Getting up slowly and wearily.*) I thought we agreed we were going to lead an active social life. Open house.

TESMAN. My God, yes, I was really looking forward to that. Seeing you as hostess at the head of your chosen circle. Mm? Yes. Ah, well, for the time being, we shall have to make do with each other, Hedda. And Auntie Julia will be able to come round quite often. But things ought to have been very different for you, very different.

HEDDA. I suppose I shan't be able to have my butler, that'll be the first thing.

TESMAN. I'm afraid not. I'm afraid servants are completely out of the question.

HEDDA. And the horse I was going to have . . .

TESMAN. (*Appalled.*) Horse?

HEDDA. . . . I suppose I'd better put that right out of my mind.

TESMAN. Good God, yes, I think that goes without saying.

HEDDA. (*Crossing the room.*) Well, anyway, I still have one diversion to keep me going while I'm waiting.

TESMAN. (*Beaming.*) Well, I'm very glad to hear it. What's that, Hedda? Mm?

HEDDA. (*In the doorway, watching him with concealed contempt.*) My pistols, George.

TESMAN. (*Anxiously.*) Your pistols?

HEDDA. (*With cold eyes.*) General Gabler's pistols. (*Exits* L. *through the back room.*)

TESMAN. (*Running over to the door and calling after her.*) No, Hedda, my dear, for God's sake, don't play with those dangerous things, don't, Hedda, for my sake, mm?

ACT TWO

The TESMANS' *room, just as it was in Act One, except that the grand piano has been moved out and replaced by an elegant little writing table with bookshelves. A small table stands next to the sofa on the* L. *Most of the flowers have been taken away.* MRS. ELVSTED'S *flowers are on the large table in the foreground.*

Afternoon. HEDDA, *dressed to receive visitors, is alone in the room. She is standing by the open glass door, loading one of her pistols. The other is lying in an open pistol-case on the writing-table.*

HEDDA. (*Looking down into the garden and calling out.*) Hello, Judge, back again!

BRACK. (*Calling from a distance.*) That's right, Mrs. Tesman.

HEDDA. (*Lifting the pistol and aiming.*) I think I'll shoot you, Judge Brack.

BRACK. (*Calling, still invisible.*) Stop it! Don't stand there pointing that thing at me.

HEDDA. This is what comes of trying to creep in the back way. (*Fires.*)

BRACK. (*Closer.*) Have you gone quite mad . . . ?

HEDDA. I didn't hit you. Or did I?

BRACK. (*Still outside.*) I wish you wouldn't fool about like that.

HEDDA. Come in, Judge.

(JUDGE BRACK, *dressed for his bachelor party, comes in through the glass door. He carries a light overcoat over his arm.*)

BRACK. My God, I thought you'd given up that game. What are you shooting at?

HEDDA. Oh, I'm just standing here, firing into the blue.

BRACK. (*Gently taking the pistol from her hand.*) Allow me. (*Looks at it.*) Ah, yes, I know this one well.

(Looks around.) Where's its case? Ah. *(Puts the pistol in the case and closes it.)* No more jokes today.

HEDDA. Well, for God's sake, what do you suggest I do with myself?

BRACK. Haven't there been any visitors?

HEDDA. *(Closing the glass door.)* Not one. All our best friends are still in the country.

BRACK. And Tesman's not at home, is he?

HEDDA. *(At the writing table, putting the pistol in a drawer and locking it.)* No. As soon as he'd eaten, he rushed over to see his aunts. He didn't expect you so early.

BRACK. Ah, why didn't I think of that? How stupid of me.

HEDDA. *(Turning to look at him.)* Stupid? Why?

BRACK. Because if I had thought of it, I could have come . . . even earlier.

HEDDA. *(Crossing the room.)* There wouldn't have been anyone here if you had. I've been in my room since lunch, changing.

BRACK. Isn't there some sort of a chink in your door, so we could at least have had a conversation?

HEDDA. You forgot to arrange for one.

BRACK. That was stupid of me as well.

HEDDA. So we'll just have to settle down here. And wait. Tesman probably won't be home for some time.

BRACK. I expect I shall manage to be patient.

(HEDDA *sits in the corner of the sofa.* BRACK *puts his overcoat over the back of the nearest chair and sits down, keeping his hat in his hands. A short silence. They look at each other.*)

HEDDA. Well?

BRACK. *(In the same tone.)* Well?

HEDDA. I asked first.

BRACK. *(Bending forward a little.)* Now, let's just have a nice quiet little chat, Hedda.

HEDDA. (*Leaning further back on the sofa.*) It seems endless ages since we last had a talk, doesn't it? Except for a few words yesterday evening and this morning, and I don't count that.

BRACK. Just the two of us, you mean? A private talk.

HEDDA. Yes. Something like that.

BRACK. Every day, when I walked past, I wished you were home again.

HEDDA. And I've spent my whole time wishing the same thing.

BRACK. Have you? Really, Hedda? I thought you were having the most wonderful time abroad.

HEDDA. Is that what you thought?

BRACK. Well, that's what Tesman said in his letters.

HEDDA. Him! His idea of bliss is rooting around in libraries. And sitting copying out old parchments, or whatever you call them.

BRACK. (*Slightly malicious.*) Well, I suppose that's what he's been called to do in life. Among other things.

HEDDA. Yes, of course. And I suppose if that's your . . . But what about me? My dear, I've been so desperately bored.

BRACK. (*Sympathetically.*) Have you really? Seriously?

HEDDA. Well, just think about it a minute. Six whole months without meeting anyone who knew anything about our friends. Or anyone who could talk about the things that interest us.

BRACK. Yes, I should think I would feel a bit cut off.

HEDDA. But the thing I found most . . . most unbearable . . .

BRACK. Yes?

HEDDA. Was always the whole time being with . . . the same one person.

BRACK. (*Nodding in agreement.*) From morning to night. Yes, I can imagine. All the time.

HEDDA. That's what I said, the whole time.

BRACK. Quite. But he's fairly innocuous, Tesman. I'd have thought you could have . . .

HEDDA. Tesman is . . . an academic.

BRACK. Undeniably.

HEDDA. And academics certainly don't make entertaining traveling companions. Not in the long run, anyway.

BRACK. Not even . . . the academic you love?

HEDDA. Ugh, please don't use that nauseating word.

BRACK. (*Surprised.*) What's that, Hedda?

HEDDA. (*Half-laughing, half-angry.*) You just try it. Listening to the history of civilization from morning to night.

BRACK. The whole time.

HEDDA. Yes. And all that stuff about medieval husbandry. That's really grim, you can't get much worse than that.

BRACK. (*Looking inquiringly at her.*) But, then, tell me . . . I mean, I don't really understand why, erm . . .

HEDDA. Why I married George Tesman?

BRACK. Well, if you like, yes.

HEDDA. Do you find it as surprising as that?

BRACK. Yes and no, Hedda.

HEDDA. I'd really danced myself to a standstill, Judge. My time was up! (*A slight shudder.*) No, I mustn't say things like that. Or think them either.

BRACK. You've certainly no reason to.

HEDDA. Ah, reasons. (*Watches him carefully.*) One thing about George Tesman, you must admit he's entirely respectable.

BRACK. Respectable and upright. God, yes.

HEDDA. And I can't think of anything really ridiculous about him, can you?

BRACK. Ridiculous? No, I don't think so, not really.

HEDDA. Well then. And he's extremely conscientious about his research work. I don't see why he shouldn't go quite a long way eventually.

BRACK. (*Looking at her a little uncertainly.*) Everyone else expects him to finish up in some exceptionally distinguished position. I thought you did too.

HEDDA. (*With a tired expression.*) Yes, I did. And

since what he seemed intent on, under any circumstances, was to look after me, I could see no reason to turn him down.

BRACK. No, well, I suppose if you look at it that way . . .

HEDDA. More than any of my other admirers were prepared to do, my dear.

BRACK. (*Laughing.*) Well, I certainly can't answer for all the others. But as far as I'm concerned, I've always felt, as you well know, a certain . . . respect for the bonds of matrimony. Generally speaking, anyway.

HEDDA. (*Lightly.*) Oh, I can assure you, I never pinned any hopes on you.

BRACK. All I want is a warm, friendly environment, where I can make myself useful in all sorts of ways, and be free to come and go and know I was . . . liked and trusted.

HEDDA. By the man of the house, you mean?

BRACK. (*Bowing.*) Well, to be quite frank, preferably by the lady. By the man as well, obviously. You see, something like that . . . what I mean is, a triangular friendship like that is really very restful for everyone concerned.

HEDDA. Yes, I don't know how often I must have longed for a third person to join us while we were away. God, those endless train compartment discussions!

BRACK. Fortunately, your honeymoon is over now. Journey's end.

HEDDA. (*Shaking her head.*) There's still a long, long way to go. This is only a station on the line.

BRACK. Well, then, you must jump out. And get some exercise, Hedda.

HEDDA. I never jump out.

BRACK. Don't you? Really?

HEDDA. No. Because there's always someone there . . .

BRACK. (*Laughing.*) Trying to see your legs, is that it?

HEDDA. Exactly.

BRACK. Yes, but . . .

HEDDA. (*Rejecting this with a gesture.*) I'm not having it. I'd rather stay where I already am. And carry on with the discussions.

BRACK. Suppose a third person were to get on and join the other two?

HEDDA. Well, now, that would be quite another matter.

BRACK. A trusted, understanding friend . . .

HEDDA. . . . able to talk about all kinds of amusing subjects . . .

BRACK. . . . and not remotely academic.

HEDDA. (*Sighing audibly.*) Well, that would certainly be a relief.

BRACK. (*Hearing the front door open and glancing toward it.*) The triangle is completed.

HEDDA. (*Half-aloud.*) And the train moves on.

(GEORGE TESMAN, *wearing a gray sports suit and a soft felt hat, enters from the hall. He carries a number of unbound books under his arm and in his pockets.*)

TESMAN. (*Moving toward the table by the corner sofa.*) Hoo, warm work lugging this lot around. (*He puts the books down.*) I'm dripping with sweat, Hedda. Ah, well, well, Judge, you're already here, are you? Mm? Berte didn't say.

BRACK. (*Getting up.*) I came in through the garden.

HEDDA. What are those books you've got?

TESMAN. (*Standing looking through them.*) Just some new books and periodicals I must catch up on. Academic stuff, you know.

HEDDA. Academic stuff?

BRACK. Ah, Mrs. Tesman, academic stuff. (BRACK *and* HEDDA *exchange understanding smiles.*)

HEDDA. How many more books and periodicals do you have to read?

BRACK. Well, my dear, there's really no limit to it. I have to keep up with everything that's written and published.

HEDDA. Yes, I suppose so.

TESMAN. (*Looking through the books.*) And look, I've managed to get hold of Eilert Lovborg's new book as well. (*Offers it to her.*) Perhaps you'd like to have a look at it, Hedda? Mm?

HEDDA. No, thanks. Well, later perhaps.

TESMAN. I had a quick look at it on the way home.

BRACK. And what do you think of it? I mean from an academic point of view.

TESMAN. Seems remarkably sound to me. He's never written like that before. (*Collects his books.*) I'll just take these into my study. I always enjoy cutting the pages so much. And then I must change. (*To* BRACK.) We don't need to leave just yet, do we? Mm?

BRACK. Oh, good Lord, no, no hurry.

TESMAN. Good, then I'll take my time. (*Takes the books with him, stops in the doorway and turns around.*) By the way, Hedda, Auntie Julia can't come and see you this evening.

HEDDA. Can't she? Nothing to do with that business about her hat, is it?

TESMAN. Not at all. I don't know how you can think a thing like that about Auntie Julia, extraordinary. No, what's happened is that Auntie Rina is very ill.

HEDDA. That's usual, isn't it?

TESMAN. Yes, but today she was really quite a lot worse, poor thing.

HEDDA. Well then, naturally her sister would want to stay and look after her. And I shall just have to put up with it.

TESMAN. Anyway, you can't imagine how delighted Auntie Julia was to see you looking so strapping after your travels.

HEDDA. (*Half-aloud, getting up.*) Oh, these endless aunts!

TESMAN. Mm?

HEDDA. (*Moving toward the glass door.*) Nothing.

TESMAN. Right. (*Exits through the back room.*)

BRACK. What hat was that you were talking about?

HEDDA. Miss Tesman's, that was something that happened this morning. She put her hat down over there on the chair . . . (*Looks at him and smiles.*) . . . and I pretended I thought it was the maid's.

BRACK. (*Shaking his head.*) But, Hedda, how could you do a thing like that? To a harmless old lady?

HEDDA. (*Crossing the room nervously.*) I don't know. I get these sudden impulses. And there's nothing I can do about it. (*Flops down onto the armchair by the stove.*) I can't explain why.

BRACK. (*Behind the armchair.*) You aren't really very happy. That's why.

HEDDA. (*Looking in front of her.*) I can't see any reason why I should be. Happy. Can you think of a reason?

BRACK. Yes. Several. For one thing here you are in the house you wanted so much.

HEDDA. (*Looking up at him and laughing.*) You don't believe in that myth as well, do you?

BRACK. Isn't it true?

HEDDA. Well, there is some truth in it.

BRACK. Go on.

HEDDA. Well, it's true that I used Tesman to escort me home after dinner parties last summer.

BRACK. Unfortunately, I had to go in a completely different direction.

HEDDA. Yes, I know you were going in different directions, last summer.

BRACK. (*Laughing.*) Really, Hedda, you ought to be ashamed of yourself. Anyway, go on about Tesman.

HEDDA. Well, we came past here one evening. And there was poor Tesman writhing about as usual, groping around trying to think of something to say. So I felt sorry for the man of learning . . .

BRACK. (*A doubting smile.*) You did, did you?

HEDDA. Yes, I did. Really. And to help him out of his misery, I just said, quite frivolously, that I'd like to live in this villa.

BRACK. Was that all you said?

HEDDA. Then, yes.

BRACK. And afterwards?

HEDDA. Afterwards, my dear, my frivolity led to other things.

BRACK. Unfortunately, Hedda, frivolity often does.

HEDDA. Thank you. So you see it was my love for Senator Falk's villa that forged the first links between George Tesman and me. And that was what led to the engagement and the wedding and the honeymoon and all the rest of it. Still, what is it they say, Judge? You've made your bed, now you must lie on it.

BRACK. How priceless! You mean you really couldn't care less about this place?

HEDDA. God, no.

BRACK. Even though we've made it so comfortable for you?

HEDDA. Ugh, all the rooms stink of lavender and dried roses. Perhaps Auntie Julia brought the smell with her.

BRACK. (*Laughing.*) More likely to be a leftover from the late Mrs. Falk.

HEDDA. Yes, there is something posthumous about it. Like flowers the morning after the ball. (*Clasps her hands behind her neck, leans back in her chair and looks at him.*) Oh, Judge, you can't imagine how terribly bored I'm going to be here.

BRACK. Why shouldn't we find something to keep you interested, Hedda, some kind of vocation?

HEDDA. Vocation? That would interest me?

BRACK. Well, preferably, yes.

HEDDA. God knows where you'd go to look for that! I often think . . . (*Breaks off.*) But I don't suppose that would work either.

BRACK. It might, tell me.

HEDDA. I was just thinking I might get Tesman to go into politics.

BRACK. (*Laughing.*) Tesman? Are you serious? Politics, he'd be hopeless at it, it wouldn't suit him at all.

HEDDA. No, I know, you're probably right. All the same I wish I could manage it for him.

BRACK. Why? What satisfaction would it give you? He wouldn't be any good at it. So why should you want to force him into it?

HEDDA. Because I'm bored, don't you understand? (*Pause.*) So you think it would be completely impossible for Tesman to become a minister?

BRACK. Erm, well, Hedda, you must realize, for one thing, even if he wanted to, he'd need to be comparatively rich.

HEDDA. (*Getting up impatiently.*) Yes, that's just it, isn't it! It's this miserable penny-pinching I've let myself in for . . . (*Crosses the room.*) That's what makes life so utterly pathetic and absurd. Because it is.

BRACK. I don't think I'd blame that for it.

HEDDA. What then?

BRACK. It's that you've never had a really rousing experience.

HEDDA. You mean something important?

BRACK. You could put it like that. And you may be about to.

HEDDA. (*Tossing her head back.*) If you mean the complications about that wretched professorship, that's Tesman's business, not mine. I'm not going to waste my time worrying about it.

BRACK. No, no, never mind about that. But suppose you were to find yourself with what might euphemistically be described as an important and . . . heavy responsibility? (*Smiles.*) A new responsibility for little Hedda.

HEDDA. (*Angrily.*) Be quiet. You won't see anything like that happen, ever.

BRACK. (*Cautiously.*) We'll talk about it again in a year's time, shall we? At the most.

HEDDA. (*Shortly.*) My dear Judge, I've got no talent for that kind of thing. Or for anything responsible.

BRACK. Don't you think you should have? After all, most women have the talent and the inclination . . .

HEDDA. (*By the glass door.*) I said be quiet. I often think there's only one thing in the world I have any talent for.

BRACK. (*Approaching her.*) And may I ask what that is?

HEDDA. (*Standing, looking out.*) Boring myself to death. Now you know. (*Turns round, looks over toward the back room and laughs.*) Yes, I was right. Here comes the professor.

BRACK. (*Quietly warning her.*) Now, now, Hedda.

(GEORGE TESMAN, *dressed for the party and carrying his hat and gloves, enters from the* R. *through the back room.*)

TESMAN. Hedda, Eilert Lovborg hasn't sent a message saying he isn't coming, has he? Mm?

HEDDA. No.

TESMAN. Then I expect he'll be here any minute.

BRACK. Do you really think he's going to come?

TESMAN. I'm almost sure he will. What you told us this morning is nothing but idle gossip.

BRACK. Is it?

TESMAN. Well, anyway, Auntie Julia told me she didn't think he'd ever get in my way again. You see?

BRACK. Oh well, that's all right, then.

TESMAN. (*Putting his hat and gloves on a chair on the* R.) Yes, well, I think if you don't mind I'd better wait for him as long as possible.

BRACK. Plenty of time. I'm not expecting anyone before seven or half-past.

TESMAN. Good, we can stay and keep Hedda company for a bit. And see what happens. Mm?

HEDDA. (*Moving* BRACK'S *overcoat and hat to the corner sofa.*) Well, if the worst comes to the worst, Mr. Lovborg can always stay here with me.

BRACK. (*Trying to take his things.*) I'll do that, Mrs. Tesman. What do you mean if the worst comes to the worst?

HEDDA. Well, if he doesn't want to go with you and Tesman.

TESMAN. (*Dubiously.*) But, Hedda dear, I don't know if it would be altogether right for him to stay here with you, do you think, mm? Auntie Julia can't come, remember?

HEDDA. Yes, but Mrs. Elvsted is coming. The three of us can have a cup of tea together.

TESMAN. Oh, well, that'll be all right.

BRACK. (*Smiling.*) Probably safer for him as well.

HEDDA. Why?

BRACK. Good Lord, Mrs. Tesman, you've made enough withering remarks in the past about my little bachelor parties. You always used to say they should only be attended by men of the very toughest moral fibre.

HEDDA. I should think Mr. Lovborg's moral fibre should be tough enough by now. He is a converted sinner.

(BERTE *appears in the hall doorway.*)

BERTE. Madam, there's a gentleman here to see you.

HEDDA. Yes, show him in.

TESMAN. (*Quietly.*) It's him, I'm sure it is. Extraordinary. (EILERT LOVBORG *enters from the hall. He is slim and lean, the same age as* TESMAN *but looks older and somewhat the worse for wear. His hair and beard are dark brown, his face is longish and pale, with a few red blotches on his cheekbones. He is wearing an elegant, very new, black suit, and carrying dark gloves and a silk hat. He stops just inside the door and bows abruptly. He seems a little embarrassed. Going up to him and shaking hands.*) Eilert, my dear chap, how nice to see you after all this time.

LOVBORG. (*Subdued.*) Thanks for your letter. (*Approaches* HEDDA.) May I shake hands with you as well, Mrs. Tesman?

HEDDA. We're delighted to see you, Mr. Lovborg. (*A gesture.*) I don't know if you two . . .

LOVBORG. (*Bowing slightly.*) Judge Brack, isn't it?

BRACK. (*The same.*) Well. It's been some time . . .

TESMAN. (*To* LOVBORG, *putting his hands on his shoulders.*) Now you must make yourself completely at home, Eilert. Mustn't he, Hedda? I gather you're planning to settle in town again, aren't you? Mm?

LOVBORG. I'd like to.

TESMAN. Very wise. Listen, I've managed to get hold of your book. But I haven't had time to read it yet

LOVBORG. I should save yourself the trouble.

TESMAN. What do you mean? Why?

LOVBORG. Because it isn't much good.

TESMAN. Extraordinary thing to say.

BRACK. But I thought it had been very well received.

LOVBORG. I intended it to be. So when I wrote the book, I made sure everyone would be able to follow it.

BRACK. Sounds reasonable.

TESMAN. Yes, but, Eilert . . .

LOVBORG. Because now I want to try to build myself up a position again. And make a fresh start.

TESMAN. (*Slightly embarrassed.*) Ah, that's it, is it? Mm?

LOVBORG. (*Smiling, putting down his hat and taking a parcel wrapped in paper from his coat pocket.*) But you must read this one, George Tesman, when it comes out. Because this is a real book. The first one I've put myself into.

TESMAN. Is it? What's it about?

LOVBORG. It's the sequel.

TESMAN. Sequel? What of?

LOVBORG. My book.

TESMAN. Your new book?

LOVBORG. That's right.

TESMAN. Yes, but, Eilert, I thought that covered everything up to the present day.

LOVBORG. It does. This one's about the future.

TESMAN. The future? But, I mean, we don't know anything about that.

LOVBORG. No. Even so, there are one or two things we can say about it. (*Opens the parcel.*) Here, have a look.

TESMAN. That's not your writing.

LOVBORG. I dictated it. (*Looks through the pages.*) It's about the future of civilization. In two parts. The first part is about the influences working on it, and this second part here . . . (*Goes on sorting through the pages.*) . . . is about the effects they'll have on its development.

TESMAN. Extraordinary. It would never occur to me to write about anything like that.

HEDDA. (*By the glass door, drumming on the pane.*) No.

LOVBORG. (*Wrapping the manuscript up again and putting the parcel on the table.*) I brought it with me because I thought I'd read some of it to you this evening.

TESMAN. Well, it was very kind of you. The only thing is . . . (*Looks at* BRACK.) I don't see how we can fit it in this evening.

LOVBORG. Never mind, some other time. There's no hurry.

BRACK. I should explain, Mr. Lovborg, we're having a little party at my house this evening. You know, in honor of Tesman really . . .

LOVBORG. (*Looking round for his hat.*) Oh, well, in that case, I won't . . .

BRACK. No, listen, I'd be very pleased if you could join us.

LOVBORG. (*Shortly and decisively.*) No, I can't. Thank you very much.

BRACK. Oh, come on. Please do. We shan't be more than a chosen few. I'm sure it'll all be very lively, as Hed— . . . um, Mrs. Tesman always says.

LOVBORG. I'm sure it will. All the same I . . .

BRACK. And you could bring your manuscript and read it to Tesman at my place. I've got plenty of rooms.

TESMAN. Yes, what about that, Eilert, you could do that, couldn't you? Mm?

HEDDA. (*Intervening.*) But suppose Mr. Lovborg doesn't want to, dear? I'm sure Mr. Lovborg would rather stay here and have dinner with me.

LOVBORG. (*Looking at her.*) With you, Mrs. Tesman?

HEDDA. And Mrs. Elvsted.

LOVBORG. Oh. (*Casually.*) Yes, I saw her for a minute this morning.

HEDDA. Did you? Yes, she's coming over. So that means you're more or less obliged to stay, Mr. Lovborg. Otherwise, she'll have no one to see her home.

LOVBORG. I see. All right, thank you very much, Mrs. Tesman, I will stay.

HEDDA. I'll just go and tell the maid. (*Goes over to the hall door and rings.*)

(BERTE *enters.* HEDDA *speaks quietly to her, pointing toward the back room.* BERTE *nods and exits.*)

TESMAN. (*While this is going on.*) Erm, Eilert, is it this new subject, I mean all this about the future, that you're going to lecture on?

LOVBORG. Yes.

TESMAN. They told me in the bookshop you were going to give a course of lectures this autumn.

LOVBORG. Yes, I am. You can't really blame me for accepting that.

TESMAN. No, of course not, my God. It's just that . . .

LOVBORG. I can see you must find it rather upsetting.

TESMAN. (*Dejectedly.*) I could hardly expect you to . . . erm, just for my sake . . .

LOVBORG. But I shall wait until you've been given your appointment.

TESMAN. Wait? Yes, but . . . yes, but . . . isn't there going to be this competition? Mm?

LOVBORG. No. . . . All I want is to outclass you. In people's minds.

TESMAN. Good heavens, Auntie Julia was right all along. I knew it, I knew it. What about that, Hedda, can you imagine, Eilert Lovborg isn't going to stand in our way.

HEDDA. Our way? It's nothing to do with me.

(*She moves toward the back room, where* BERTE *is putting a tray of decanters and glasses on the table.* HEDDA *nods approval and returns.* BERTE *exits.*)

TESMAN. (*While this is going on.*) What about you, Judge Brack, what do you think about all this? Mm?

BRACK. Well, I think winning the honor of outclassing someone is all very commendable, er . . .

TESMAN. Yes, it is. Certainly. Even so . . .

HEDDA. (*Looking at* TESMAN *and smiling coldly.*) You look as if you'd been struck by lightning.

TESMAN. Yes. I feel a bit . . . like that.

BRACK. Well, after all, a thunderstorm has just passed over us, Mrs. Tesman.

HEDDA. (*Pointing toward the back room.*) Wouldn't you all like to go in and have a glass of cold punch?

BRACK. (*Looking at his watch.*) Before we go? Wouldn't do any harm.

TESMAN. Marvelous idea, Hedda, marvelous! Now I'm in such a good mood . . .

HEDDA. And you, Mr. Lovborg, please.

LOVBORG. (*Gesture of refusal.*) No, thank you. Not for me.

BRACK. Good Lord, there's nothing poisonous about a drop of cold punch.

LOVBORG. Perhaps not for some people.

HEDDA. Never mind, I'll take care of Mr. Lovborg.

TESMAN. Yes, do, Hedda dear, would you?

(*He and* BRACK *go into the back room, sit down, drink punch, light cigarettes and talk animatedly during the following scene.* LOVBORG *remains standing by the stove.* HEDDA *goes over to the writing table.*)

HEDDA. (*In a rather loud voice.*) I'll show you some photographs, shall I, would you like that? Tesman and I passed through the Tyrol on our way home. (*Fetches an album, puts it on the table by the sofa, and then sits in the far corner of the sofa.* LOVBORG *approaches, stops and looks at her. Then he fetches a chair and sits down on her left with his back to the back room. Opening the album.*) Now. You see this mountain range here, Mr. Lovborg? It's the Ortler range. Tesman's written the names underneath. Here we are. The Ortler range. Near Meran.

LOVBORG. (*Who has been watching her carefully, now speaks quietly and slowly.*) Hedda . . . Gabler.

HEDDA. (*Looking up sharply.*) What? Ssh!

LOVBORG. (*Repeats softly.*) Hedda Gabler.

HEDDA. (*Looking at the album.*) Yes, that was my name once. When . . . you and I used to know each other.

LOVBORG. So from now on for the rest of my life I must learn to stop saying Hedda Gabler.

HEDDA. (*Continuing to turn the pages.*) Yes, you must. And I think you ought to start practising. The sooner the better, I'd say.

LOVBORG. (*Indignantly.*) Hedda Gabler married. And to George Tesman!

HEDDA. Yes. That's the way things happen.

LOVBORG. Oh, Hedda, Hedda, how could you throw yourself away like that?

HEDDA. (*Looking at him sharply.*) What? That's enough of that.

LOVBORG. What do you mean?

(TESMAN *enters and approaches the sofa.*)

HEDDA. (*Hearing him coming, adopts a neutral tone.*) And this, Mr. Lovborg, is taken from the d'Ampezzo valley. Look at those mountains. (*Looks up at* TESMAN *affectionately.*) What's the name of that peculiar range, dear?

TESMAN. Let's have a look. Oh yes, those are the Dolomites.

HEDDA. That's right. Those are the Dolomites, Mr. Lovborg.

TESMAN. Hedda, I was just wondering if you wouldn't like us to bring in some punch anyway. I mean, for you. Mm?

HEDDA. Yes, why don't you, thanks. And perhaps a few biscuits.

TESMAN. Cigarettes?

HEDDA. No.

TESMAN. Right.

(*He goes into the back room and moves across to the* R. BRACK *is sitting there and glancing from time to time at* HEDDA *and* LOVBORG.)

LOVBORG. (*Quietly as before.*) Now, tell me, Hedda. How could you do a thing like this?

HEDDA. (*Pretending to be absorbed in the album.*) If you go on calling me Hedda, I shan't want to talk to you at all.

LOVBORG. Can't I even call you Hedda when we're alone?

HEDDA. No. You can think it. But you mustn't say it.

LOVBORG. I see. It's an insult to your love . . . for George Tesman, is it?

HEDDA. (*Looks at him, smiling.*) Love? Don't be ridiculous.

LOVBORG. You don't love him, then?

HEDDA. That doesn't mean I'd ever be unfaithful to him. Because I wouldn't.

LOVBORG. Just tell me one thing . . .

HEDDA. Ssh!

(TESMAN *enters from the back room with a small tray.*)

TESMAN. Here you are. Goodies. (*Puts the tray down on the table.*)

HEDDA. Why are you serving it yourself?

TESMAN. (*Filling the glasses.*) I think it's such fun doing things for you, Hedda.

HEDDA. Now you've filled both glasses. Mr. Lovborg doesn't want any.

TESMAN. No, but Mrs. Elvsted will probably be here soon.

HEDDA. Oh, yes, Mrs. Elvsted . . .

TESMAN. You hadn't forgotten her, had you? Mm?

HEDDA. We've been so engrossed in this. (*Shows him a photo.*) Do you remember that little village?

TESMAN. Oh, yes, it's the one at the bottom of the Brenner Pass. Where we spent the night . . .

HEDDA. . . . and met all those lively summer visitors.

TESMAN. Yes, that's right. I only wish you'd been with us then, Eilert. Yes. (*Goes into the back room and sits down with* BRACK *again.*)

LOVBORG. Will you just tell me one thing . . .

HEDDA. What?

LOVBORG. Was there no love in your feeling for me either? Was there no trace, no spark of love at all?

HEDDA. I don't know. I saw us as two loyal companions. Two really close friends. (*Smiles.*) I remember you were always very candid.

LOVBORG. That was what you wanted.

HEDDA. When I look back on it, I often feel there was something beautiful and appealing and . . . and brave . . . about our secret closeness and about having a friendship that no one in the world had any idea of.

LOVBORG. Yes, there was, wasn't there? I used to come and spend the afternoon at your father's. And the general used to sit by the window, reading the paper. With his back to us.

HEDDA. And we used to sit on the sofa in the corner . . .

LOVBORG. Always with the same magazine open in front of us.

HEDDA. Not having a photograph album.

LOVBORG. Yes. And I used to make my confession to

you. And tell you things about myself that no one else knew anything about. Used to sit there admitting I'd been out celebrating all day and night. Always to excess. What kind of power did you have over me to make me want to confide in you like that?

HEDDA. Did I have any power over you?

LOVBORG. Yes, I can't explain it any other way. And all those . . . enigmatic questions you used to ask me . . .

HEDDA. Which you always understood immediately . . .

LOVBORG. How could you sit there and ask me questions like that? Quite openly?

HEDDA. Enigmatically, you just said.

LOVBORG. Yes, but openly as well. Asking me about all those things.

HEDDA. How could you answer, Mr. Lovborg?

LOVBORG. Well, exactly, when I think about it now, I can't understand it either. Tell me, wasn't love the basis of our friendship? Didn't you want to absolve me when I came to confess to you? Wasn't that it?

HEDDA. Not quite, no.

LOVBORG. What were your motives, then?

HEDDA. Do you really find it so difficult to understand? A young girl, given the chance, with no danger of being found out . . .

LOVBORG. Yes?

HEDDA. . . . wanting to catch a glimpse of a world. . . .

LOVBORG. Go on.

HEDDA. . . . a world she's not allowed to know anything about.

LOVBORG. So that was it?

HEDDA. That was part of it. Something like that.

LOVBORG. Sympathy for my attitude to life. Why shouldn't you, at least, have kept that?

HEDDA. That was your fault.

LOVBORG. You finished it.

HEDDA. Yes, because there was a growing danger that our relationship would turn into something more serious.

You should be ashamed, Eilert Lovborg. How could you try to take advantage of your . . . trusting friend?

LOVBORG. (*Clenching his fists.*) Why didn't you do it? You threatened to shoot me, why didn't you?

HEDDA. Because I'm terrified of scandal.

LOVBORG. Yes, Hedda. You're a coward, really, aren't you?

HEDDA. A dreadful coward. (*Change of tone.*) Luckily for you. Anyway, I see you've found true consolation at the Elvsteds'.

LOVBORG. I know Thea has confided in you.

HEDDA. And I expect you've confided in her. About us.

LOVBORG. I haven't said a word. She's too stupid to understand a thing like that.

HEDDA. Stupid?

LOVBORG. Stupid about that kind of thing.

HEDDA. And I'm a coward. (*Leans toward him, avoiding his eyes and speaks more quietly.*) But now I'm going to confide something to you.

LOVBORG. (*Eagerly.*) What?

HEDDA. My not daring to shoot you . . .

LOVBORG. Yes?

HEDDA. . . . wasn't my most cowardly failure . . . that evening.

LOVBORG. (*Looking at her for a moment before understanding and whispering passionately.*) Oh, Hedda! Hedda Gabler! So there was something hidden behind our friendship, I can see that now. You and I . . . You were longing for life as well.

HEDDA. (*Quietly, with a sharp glance.*) Be careful. Don't jump to any conclusions. (*It is getting dark.* BERTE *opens the hall door from the outside. Snapping the album shut, smiling and calling out.*) At last! Thea, my dear, come in. (MRS. ELVSTED *enters from the hall. She is wearing a party dress. The door is closed behind her. From the sofa, stretching her arms out toward her.*) Thea, I've been longing to see you.

(MRS. ELVSTED *exchanges brief greetings with the men in the back room as she passes, crosses to the table and shakes hands with* HEDDA. LOVBORG *has stood up. He and* MRS. ELVSTED *acknowledge each other with a silent nod.*)

MRS. ELVSTED. Perhaps I should go and have a word with your husband?

HEDDA. I shouldn't. I should leave them alone. They'll be going soon.

MRS. ELVSTED. Going?

HEDDA. Yes, they're going out on a drinking bout.

MRS. ELVSTED. (*Quickly to* LOVBORG.) You're not going, are you?

LOVBORG. No.

HEDDA. Mr. Lovborg's staying here with us.

MRS. ELVSTED. (*Taking a chair and preparing to sit next to him.*) It's very good to be here.

HEDDA. No, Thea, not there, please. Come over here next to me. I want to sit between you.

MRS. ELVSTED. Just as you like. (*Walks round the table and sits on the sofa on* HEDDA'S *right.* LOVBORG *sits down in his chair again.*)

LOVBORG. (*After a short pause, to* HEDDA.) Isn't she beautiful to look at?

HEDDA. (*Gently stroking her hair.*) Only to look at?

LOVBORG. Yes. The two of us, she and I, are real friends. We trust each other implicitly. It means we can sit and discuss things really openly. . . .

HEDDA. No secrets, Mr. Lovborg, no . . . enigmas?

LOVBORG. Well . . .

MRS. ELVSTED. (*Softly, clinging on to* HEDDA.) I'm so happy, Hedda. He says I've inspired him as well.

HEDDA. (*Looking at her with a smile.*) No, does he say that?

LOVBORG. The way she does things, Mrs. Tesman, she has such courage.

MRS. ELVSTED. Courage, me!

LOVBORG. Unlimited courage, when it comes to helping your friend.

HEDDA. Ah, courage. If only I had some.

LOVBORG. What do you mean?

HEDDA. Then perhaps life would be worth living. (*Changes the subject abruptly.*) Now, Thea dear, you must have a nice glass of cold punch.

MRS. ELVSTED. No, thank you, I don't.

HEDDA. Well, what about you, Mr. Lovborg?

LOVBORG. No, thanks, I don't either.

MRS. ELVSTED. He doesn't either.

HEDDA. (*Looking at him hard.*) What if I wanted you to?

LOVBORG. Wouldn't make any difference.

HEDDA. (*Laughing.*) Poor me, haven't I got any influence over you at all?

LOVBORG. Not as far as this is concerned.

HEDDA. I still think you should. Seriously. For your sake.

MRS. ELVSTED. Hedda . . .

LOVBORG. Why?

HEDDA. Or rather for other people's sake.

LOVBORG. What do you mean?

HEDDA. Otherwise people might get the impression that secretly you're not really being very honest, and that you haven't really got any confidence in yourself.

MRS. ELVSTED. (*Quietly.*) Hedda, don't . . .

LOVBORG. They can think what they like.

MRS. ELVSTED. (*Fnthusiastically.*) Yes!

HEDDA. It's just that looking at Judge Brack a moment ago, I could see it so clearly.

LOVBORG. See what?

HEDDA. The contempt in his smile when you didn't dare join them in there.

LOVBORG. Didn't dare? Obviously I preferred to stay here and talk to you.

MRS. ELVSTED. There's nothing surprising about that, is there, Hedda?

HEDDA. No, but that wouldn't be likely to occur to Judge Brack. And I also noticed he couldn't help smiling and catching Tesman's eye when you didn't dare agree to go to his miserable little party.

LOVBORG. Didn't dare? Do you think I didn't dare?

HEDDA. I don't. But that's what Judge Brack thought.

LOVBORG. Well, let him.

HEDDA. So you're not going then?

LOVBORG. I'm staying here with you and Thea.

MRS. ELVSTED. Of course he is, Hedda.

HEDDA. (*Smiling and nodding at* LOVBORG.) Solid foundations. Principles firm to the last. That's how a man should be. (*Turns to* MRS. ELVSTED, *caressing her.*) You see, isn't that what I told you this morning, when you came in so upset . . . ?

LOVBORG. (*Taken aback.*) Upset?

MRS. ELVSTED. (*Terrified.*) Hedda . . .

HEDDA. You can see now, can't you? There was no need for all that desperate worry . . . (*Breaks off.*) And now, let's enjoy ourselves, shall we?

LOVBORG. (*Shuddering.*) Oh, what is all this, Mrs. Tesman?

MRS. ELVSTED. Oh, God, Hedda! What are you saying? What are you doing?

HEDDA. Calm down. That abominable Judge is sitting staring at you.

LOVBORG. Desperate worry. About me.

MRS. ELVSTED. (*Quietly, miserably.*) Oh, Hedda, you've made me terribly unhappy.

LOVBORG. (*Looking at her intently for a moment, face contorted.*) That's what we call a friend's implicit trust.

MRS. ELVSTED. (*Imploringly.*) Just listen to me for a minute. . . .

LOVBORG. (*Taking one of the full glasses of punch, raising it and speaking quietly and hoarsely.*) Here's to you, Thea! (*Empties the glass, puts it down and takes the other.*)

MRS. ELVSTED. (*Quietly.*) Oh, Hedda, why should you want this to happen?

HEDDA. Me? Want it? Are you mad?

LOVBORG. And here's to you, Mrs. Tesman. Thank you for telling me the truth. Here's to the truth! (*Drinks and goes to fill the glass again.*)

HEDDA. (*Putting her hand on his arm.*) No more just now. Remember you're going out to dinner.

MRS. ELVSTED. No, no, he isn't!

HEDDA. Ssh! They're looking at you.

LOVBORG. (*Putting the glass down.*) Now, Thea . . . tell me the truth now . . .

MRS. ELVSTED. Yes.

LOVBORG. Did your husband know you'd come after me?

MRS. ELVSTED. (*Wringing her hands.*) Oh, Hedda, did you hear what he said?

LOVBORG. Was it something you worked out between you, your coming into town to watch over me? Or perhaps it was the sheriff's idea, perhaps he persuaded you to come? He probably needed me in his office, is that it? Or did he miss me at the card table?

MRS. ELVSTED. (*Quietly, suffering.*) Oh, Lovborg . . .

LOVBORG. (*Picking up the glass and moving to fill it.*) Here's to the old sheriff while we're at it.

HEDDA. (*Preventing him.*) No more now. Remember you're going out and you're going to read your book to Tesman.

LOVBORG. (*Calm, putting the glass down.*) That was stupid of me, Thea, just now. Reacting like that, I mean. Don't be angry with me, my dear friend. You'll see, you and the others, even if I was far gone once, now, I've pulled myself back. With your help, Thea.

MRS. ELVSTED. (*Glowing.*) Thank God . . . !

(*In the meantime,* BRACK *has consulted his watch. He and* TESMAN *rise and move into the drawing room.*)

BRACK. (*Taking his hat and overcoat.*) Well, Mrs. Tesman, time we were on our way.

HEDDA. I suppose it is.

LOVBORG. (*Getting up.*) I'll come with you, Judge Brack. . . .

MRS. ELVSTED. (*Quietly and imploringly.*) Don't, Lovborg, please. . . .

HEDDA. (*Pinching her arm.*) They can hear you!

MRS. ELVSTED. (*A faint cry.*) Ow!

LOVBORG. (*To* BRACK.) . . . as you were kind enough to invite me.

BRACK. Changed your mind, then?

LOVBORG. Yes, if that's all right with you.

BRACK. Good, I'm delighted.

LOVBORG. (*Picking up his parcel; to* TESMAN.) There are one or two things I'd like to show you before I send it in.

TESMAN. Well, that'll be very interesting. The only thing is, Hedda, how are we going to get Mrs. Elvsted home? Mm?

HEDDA. Oh, I'm sure we'll manage.

LOVBORG. (*Looking over at the women.*) Mrs. Elvsted? Obviously I must come back and collect her. (*Approaches.*) About ten o'clock, Mrs. Tesman? Will that be all right?

HEDDA. Yes, of course. Perfectly all right.

TESMAN. Well, then, that's arranged. But you mustn't expect me that early, Hedda.

HEDDA. My dear, you can stay as long . . . as long as you like.

MRS. ELVSTED. (*Trying to conceal her anxiety.*) So I'll . . . wait for you here, shall I, Mr. Lovborg?

LOVBORG. (*Hat in hand.*) That's right, Mrs. Elvsted.

BRACK. So, gentlemen, the mystery train is pulling out. I'm hoping it'll all be very lively, as a certain charming lady always says.

HEDDA. I wish that charming lady could be there, invisible.

BRACK. Why invisible?

HEDDA. To hear some of your lively conversations unabridged, Judge.

BRACK. (*Laughing.*) I really wouldn't recommend that to any charming lady.

TESMAN. (*Also laughing.*) My word, Hedda, that's a good one! Extraordinary.,

BRACK. Well, good-bye, ladies.

LOVBORG. (*Bowing as he leaves.*) See you about ten.

(BRACK, LOVBORG *and* TESMAN *leave by the hall door. At the same time* BERTE *enters from the back room with a lighted lamp, which she puts on the living-room table before exiting the same way.*)

MRS. ELVSTED. (*Having got up, pacing restlessly around the room.*) Hedda, what's going to happen now?

HEDDA. Ten o'clock. He'll be here. I can see him now. Vine leaves in his hair. Burning with courage.

MRS. ELVSTED. I hope so.

HEDDA. And, don't you see, then he'll be in control of himself again. And he'll be a free man for the rest of his life.

MRS. ELVSTED. Oh, God, I only hope you're right.

HEDDA. It'll all be exactly as I say. (*Gets up and moves nearer to* THEA.) You can doubt him as much as you like. I believe in him. And now we shall see which of us is right.

MRS. ELVSTED. You must have some ulterior motive in all this, Hedda.

HEDDA. Yes, I have. For once in my life I want the power to control a human destiny.

MRS. ELVSTED. Haven't you got that?

HEDDA. No, I haven't. I never have had.

MRS. ELVSTED. What about your husband?

HEDDA. Do you really think he's worth the effort? I wish you could understand how poor I am. And you've finished up so rich. (*Puts her arms round her passionately.*) I think I shall set fire to your hair after all.

MRS. ELVSTED. Let go! Let me go! I'm frightened of you, Hedda.

BERTE. (*In the doorway.*) Tea's ready in the dining room, madam.

HEDDA. Good. We're coming.

MRS. ELVSTED. No, no, I'm not. I'd rather go home alone. Now.

HEDDA. Nonsense! You're going to have tea first, you little numbskull. And then, at ten o'clock, Eilert Lovborg will arrive . . . with vine leaves in his hair. (*Virtually forces* MRS. ELVSTED *toward the doorway.*)

ACT THREE

The TESMANS' *room. The curtains in the doorway to the back room and in front of the glass door are drawn. The lamp is on the table, turned down and shaded to give a dim light. The stove door is open and we can see the remains of a fire, which has almost burnt itself out.*

MRS. ELVSTED, *wrapped in a large shawl and resting her feet on a stool, is sitting near the stove, leaning back in an armchair.* HEDDA *is lying fully dressed on the sofa, covered by a blanket. After a pause,* MRS. ELVSTED *suddenly sits up in her chair and listens anxiously. Then she sinks back again wearily, moaning softly.*

MRS. ELVSTED. Still not back! Oh, God, God . . . still. (BERTE *tiptoes cautiously in from the hall door, carrying a letter. Turning and whispering tensely.*) Is anyone back yet?

BERTE. (*Quietly.*) Yes, a girl just arrived with this letter.

MRS. ELVSTED. (*Quickly, stretching out her hand.*) A letter? Give it to me!

BERTE. It's for the doctor, madam.

MRS. ELVSTED. Oh.

BERTE. Miss Tesman's maid brought it. I'll put it here on the table.

MRS. ELVSTED. Yes, do.

BERTE. (*Putting the letter on the table.*) I think I'd better put the lamp out. It's starting to smoke.

MRS. ELVSTED. Yes, I should. It'll soon be light.

BERTE. It is light, madam.

MRS. ELVSTED. Dawn already. And no one's back yet.

BERTE. Good Lord, no, I thought that's what it would be.

MRS. ELVSTED. Did you?

BERTE. Well, when I heard a certain gentleman had come back to town, and when he went off with them . . . We used to hear enough about him in the old days.

MRS. ELVSTED. Don't speak so loud. You'll wake up Mrs. Tesman.

BERTE. (*Looking at the sofa and sighing.*) Oh, dear, poor thing, we'll let her sleep a bit longer. Shall I put a bit more on the fire?

MRS. ELVSTED. No, thanks, I'm warm enough.

BERTE. All right. (*Exits quietly by the hall door.*)

HEDDA. (*Waking up when the door shuts and looking around.*) Who's that . . . ?

MRS. ELVSTED. Only the maid.

HEDDA. (*Looking around.*) What are . . . ? Oh, yes, I remember. (*Sits up on the sofa, stretching and rubbing her eyes.*) What time is it, Thea?

MRS. ELVSTED. (*Looking at her watch.*) After seven.

HEDDA. What time did Tesman get in?

MRS. ELVSTED. He hasn't come back yet.

HEDDA. Still not back?

MRS. ELVSTED. (*Getting up.*) No one is.

HEDDA. But we stayed up waiting till four o'clock.

MRS. ELVSTED. (*Wringing her hands.*) I've been waiting for him all night.

HEDDA. (*Yawning and speaking with her hand in front of her mouth.*) We might have saved ourselves the trouble.

MRS. ELVSTED. Did you manage to get some sleep?

HEDDA. Yes. I think I slept quite well. Didn't you?

MRS. ELVSTED. Not a wink. I couldn't, Hedda! I couldn't possibly.

HEDDA. (*Getting up and moving toward her.*) Don't worry, there's nothing to worry about. I know exactly what's happened.

MRS. ELVSTED. What? Tell me.

HEDDA. Well, presumably, it's just dragged on endlessly at the Judge's . . .

MRS. ELVSTED. Well, yes, obviously. Even so . . .

HEDDA. And I expect Tesman didn't want to come home and wake everyone up ringing the bell in the middle of the night. (*Laughs.*) He probably didn't want to show his face either . . . after all that celebrating.

MRS. ELVSTED. But . . . where else could he have gone?

HEDDA. I expect he's gone over to his aunts' and slept there. They keep his old room ready for him.

MRS. ELVSTED. No, he can't have stayed there. A letter just arrived for him from Miss Tesman. There.

HEDDA. Really? (*Looks at the handwriting on the envelope.*) Yes, that's Aunt Julia's writing. Well, he must have stayed at the Judge's, then. And Eilert Lovborg is sitting there, with vine leaves in his hair, reading aloud.

MRS. ELVSTED. Oh, Hedda, you're just saying that, you don't believe it.

HEDDA. You really are a little idiot, Thea.

MRS. ELVSTED. I'm sorry, I suppose I am.

HEDDA. You look desperately tired.

MRS. ELVSTED. Yes, I am desperately tired.

HEDDA. Well, you must take my advice. Go into my room and lie down for a bit.

MRS. ELVSTED. No, no, I couldn't sleep now.

HEDDA. Of course you can.

MRS. ELVSTED. All right, but your husband's bound to get back soon. And when he does, I want to know straightaway. . . .

HEDDA. I'll tell you as soon as he gets in.

MRS. ELVSTED. Promise, Hedda?

HEDDA. Yes, I promise. Now go in and get some sleep.

MRS. ELVSTED. Thanks. I'll try. (*Exits through the back room.*)

(HEDDA *goes over to the glass door and draws back the curtains. Daylight streams into the room. She picks up a small mirror from the writing table, looks at herself in it and tidies her hair. She goes over to the hall door and presses the bell. After a short pause,* BERTE *appears.*)

BERTE. Yes, madam?

HEDDA. Put some more wood on the stove, will you? I'm freezing.

BERTE. Won't take a minute to get warm. (*Rakes the fire and puts a block of wood on it. Standing listening.*) That was the front door, wasn't it, madam?

HEDDA. Go and answer it then. I'll look after the fire.

BERTE. It'll catch in no time. (*Exits through the hall door.*)

(HEDDA *kneels on the footstool and puts some more blocks of wood on the fire. A moment later,* TESMAN *enters from the hall. He looks tired and rather solemn. He tiptoes toward the doorway and is about to slip through the curtains.*)

HEDDA. (*Without looking up from the stove.*) Morning.

TESMAN. (*Turning.*) Hedda! (*Approaches her.*) Good gracious me, up so early? Mm?

HEDDA. Yes, I got up very early this morning.

TESMAN. Extraordinary. I was sure you'd still be in bed.

HEDDA. Don't talk so loud, Mrs. Elvsted is lying down in my room.

TESMAN. Did Mrs. Elvsted stay the night here?

HEDDA. Well, no one came to fetch her.

TESMAN. No, I suppose not.

HEDDA. (*Shutting the stove door and getting up.*) Well, did you enjoy yourself at the Judge's?

TESMAN. Were you worried about me? Mm?

HEDDA. Certainly not. I just wondered if you enjoyed yourself.

TESMAN. Yes, I did. For once. Especially at the beginning of the evening. When Eilert read to me. We arrived more than an hour early, if you can imagine. And Brack had a lot to see to. So Eilert read to me.

HEDDA. (*Sitting down on the* R. *of the table.*) Tell me about it. . . .

TESMAN. (*Sitting on the footstool by the stove.*) Oh, Hedda, you couldn't begin to imagine what that book will be like. It must be one of the most remarkable books ever written. Extraordinary.

HEDDA. No, no, I didn't really mean that. . . .

TESMAN. I'll tell you something, Hedda. When he'd finished reading, something really horrible happened to me.

HEDDA. Horrible?

TESMAN. I sat there envying Eilert for being able to write like that. Can you imagine, Hedda?

HEDDA. I can, yes.

TESMAN. And the terrible thing is that he has all that talent, and yet he's absolutely irredeemable.

HEDDA. Do you mean because he's more high-spirited than the others?

TESMAN. No, I mean because he's quite incapable of doing anything in moderation.

HEDDA. So what happened in the end?

TESMAN. Well, I think it became rather what might be described as bacchanalian.

HEDDA. And did he have vine leaves in his hair?

TESMAN. Vine leaves? I didn't notice any. But he made a long, incoherent speech about the woman who had inspired him in his work. That's how he described her, anyway.

HEDDA. Did he mention her name?

TESMAN. No, he didn't. But I can't think it could be anyone else but Mrs. Elvsted. Take my word for it.

HEDDA. Where did you leave him?

TESMAN. On the way into town. It broke up, and the last of us all left at the same time. Brack came with us to get a bit of fresh air. And in the end, you see, we agreed to take Eilert home. He had rather overdone it.

HEDDA. I suppose he had.

TESMAN. Now, this is the really strange thing, Hedda. Or perhaps tragic is a better word for it. I feel almost too ashamed, on Eilert's behalf, to tell you about it. . . .

HEDDA. Oh, get on with it. . . .

TESMAN. Well, you see, as we were coming into town, I just happened to drop back a bit behind the others. Only for a couple of minutes, if you can imagine.

HEDDA. Yes, yes, for goodness' sake . . .

TESMAN. And then, when I was hurrying to catch up with the others, do you know what I found lying on the pavement? Mm?

HEDDA. How should I know?

TESMAN. You mustn't tell anyone about this, Hedda. Do you understand? Promise you won't, for Eilert's sake. (*Takes a parcel wrapped in paper from his coat pocket.*) This is what I found. Now, what do you think?

HEDDA. Isn't that the parcel he had with him yesterday?

TESMAN. Yes, it's the whole of his priceless, irreplaceable manuscript. He'd lost it without realizing. It's extraordinary, Hedda. It's tragic. . . .

HEDDA. Why didn't you give it back to him straightaway?

TESMAN. I didn't dare. The state he was in . . .

HEDDA. You didn't tell any of the others you'd found it?

TESMAN. Of course not. I didn't want to, you see, for Eilert's sake.

HEDDA. So nobody knows that you have Eilert Lovborg's manuscript.

TESMAN. No. And nobody must find out about it either.

HEDDA. What did you say to him afterwards?

TESMAN. I didn't get a chance to say anything to him. When we got into town, he and two or three others suddenly vanished, just like that. It was extraordinary.

HEDDA. Really? They must have taken him home.

TESMAN. Yes, I suppose they must have. Brack disappeared as well.

HEDDA. And where have you been lurking about since then?

TESMAN. Well, one of our merry company invited some of us back to his place for morning coffee. Or perhaps I should say night coffee, mm? Anyway, as soon as I've had a little rest, and given Eilert a chance to sleep it off a bit, poor chap, I must go round and give this back to him.

HEDDA. (*Reaching out for the parcel.*) No, don't give it back yet. I mean, not just yet. Let me read it first.

TESMAN. No, Hedda, my dear, really, I can't do that, honestly.

HEDDA. Can't you?

TESMAN. No, surely you realize how desperate he'll be when he wakes up and finds the manuscript missing. There's no copy of it, you know. He told me there wasn't.

HEDDA. (*Looking hard at him.*) But that sort of book could be written again, couldn't it? And come out much the same.

TESMAN. No, I don't think that would ever work. It's the inspiration, you see . . .

HEDDA. Yes, I suppose you're right. . . . (*Casually.*) Incidentally, there's a letter for you.

TESMAN. There isn't, is there?

HEDDA. (*Handing it to him.*) It arrived this morning, early.

TESMAN. Oh, it's from Auntie Julia. I wonder what it is. (*Puts the parcel on the other footstool, opens the letter, reads it and leaps up.*) Oh, Hedda, she says poor Auntie Rina is dying.

HEDDA. We've been expecting that, haven't we?

TESMAN. And that if I want to see her again, I shall have to hurry. I'd better race up there this minute.

HEDDA. (*Suppressing a smile.*) On your marks.

TESMAN. I wish you could bring yourself to come with me, Hedda dear. Won't you consider it?

HEDDA. (*Getting up and speaking wearily but decisively.*) No, don't ask me to. I don't want to look at sickness and death. Or anything ugly, I don't want anything to do with it.

TESMAN. Well . . . (*Bustles around.*) Where's my hat? And my coat, where are they? Ah yes, in the hall. I only hope I won't be too late, Hedda, mm?

HEDDA. You'd better race up there . . .

(BERTE *comes in from the hall.*)

BERTE. Judge Brack is here, he wants to know if he can come in.

TESMAN. Now? No, I can't possibly see him now.

HEDDA. I can. (*To* BERTE.) Show him in. (*Exit* BERTE. *Whispering hurriedly.*) Tesman, the parcel! (*Snatches it up from the footstool.*)

TESMAN. Oh, yes, give it to me.

HEDDA. No, no, I'll look after it for you. (*She goes over to the writing table and puts the parcel on the bookshelf.* TESMAN *is in a hurry, and finding it impossible to get his gloves on.* BRACK *enters from the hall. Nodding to him.*) Well, you're an early bird, aren't you?

BRACK. Yes, I am, aren't I? (*To* TESMAN.) Are you going out?

TESMAN. Yes, I have to get up to my aunts'. One of them, the invalid, you know, poor thing, can you imagine, she's dying.

BRACK. Oh, my God, is she? You mustn't let me keep you, then. At a time like this . . .

TESMAN. Yes, I must dash, really . . . Good-bye, good-bye. (*Hurries out through the hall door.*)

HEDDA. (*Approaching.*) Well, Judge Brack, I gather things were more than lively at your party last night.

BRACK. I certainly haven't been to bed, Hedda.

HEDDA. You as well?

BRACK. As you can see. What's Tesman been telling you about the night's dramas?

HEDDA. Oh, nothing remotely interesting. Just some story about them going and having coffee somewhere.

BRACK. Yes, I've heard about their coffee party already. I understand Eilert Lovborg wasn't with them?

HEDDA. No, they took him home before that.

BRACK. Tesman took him home?

HEDDA. No, he told me some of the others did.

BRACK. You know, Hedda, George Tesman really is a trusting soul.

HEDDA. Well, God knows that's true. Why, is there something more to all this?

BRACK. I must admit that there is.

HEDDA. Well! Let's sit down, shall we, Judge? Then you can tell me about it in comfort. (*Sits at the left-hand end of the table,* BRACK *sits on the long side of the table, near her.*) Carry on.

BRACK. I had special reasons for keeping track of my guests, or rather some of my guests, last night.

HEDDA. Was one of those by any chance Eilert Lovborg?

BRACK. I must confess that he was.

HEDDA. Now you're getting me really interested. . . .

BRACK. Do you know where he and some of the others spent the rest of the night, Hedda?

HEDDA. If you feel you can tell me, I wish you would.

BRACK. Of course I can tell you. They finished up at a particularly interesting soirée.

HEDDA. Lively?

BRACK. Extremely lively.

HEDDA. You wouldn't like to enlarge on that, would you, Judge?

BRACK. In fact, Lovborg, as well as the others, had been invited to it some time ago. As I very well knew. But at that time he had refused the invitation. Because, as you know, he has recently turned himself into a new man.

HEDDA. You mean at Sheriff Elvsted's? But even so, he went?

BRACK. Yes, well, you see, Hedda, last night, at my house, I'm afraid the spirit moved him.

HEDDA. Yes, I'm told he was quite inspired.

BRACK. Tremendously inspired. To the point of violence. And that, I suppose, led on to certain other thoughts. You see, unfortunately, the thing about us men is that our principles are not always as firm as they ought to be.

HEDDA. Oh, I'm sure that doesn't apply to you, Judge Brack. Anyway, go on about Lovborg. . . .

BRACK. Well, to cut a long story short . . . he finished up at Miss Diana's apartments.

HEDDA. Miss Diana?

BRACK. It was Miss Diana who was giving the soirée. For a select group of her friends and admirers.

HEDDA. Is she a redhead?

BRACK. That's right.

HEDDA. A kind of singer?

BRACK. Yes. And appropriately enough, a mighty huntress . . . of men, Hedda. I'm sure you must have heard of her. Eilert Lovborg was one of her most energetic supporters . . . in palmier days.

HEDDA. How did it all end?

BRACK. Not altogether cordially, it seems. Miss Diana welcomed him very enthusiastically, but it seems to have ended in something of a brawl.

HEDDA. Between her and Lovborg?

BRACK. Yes. He accused her or one of her friends of stealing from him. He insisted that his notebook had disappeared. As well as various other things. In fact, he seems to have started the most terrible row.

HEDDA. And what happened then?

BRACK. What happened then was a free-for-all with women joining in as well as men. Eventually, I'm happy to say, the police arrived.

HEDDA. The police?

BRACK. Yes. It's going to be one of Eilert Lovborg's most expensive pranks. Lunatic.

HEDDA. Why do you say that?

BRACK. Apparently he resisted with some violence. Apparently he attacked one of the constables, beat him about the ears and ripped his jacket to pieces. After that, they asked him to accompany them to the station.

HEDDA. How did you find all this out?

BRACK. From the police.

HEDDA. (*Staring straight in front of her.*) So that's what happened. No vine leaves in his hair.

BRACK. Vine leaves, Hedda?

HEDDA. (*Changing her tone.*) Tell me, Judge . . . why are you so interested in keeping track of Eilert Lovborg?

BRACK. Well, in the first place, it could hardly be a matter of complete indifference to me if it were to come out in court that he'd come straight from my house.

HEDDA. There'll be a court case then, will there?

BRACK. Of course. Not that we really need to have any worries about that. No, what I thought was, that, as a friend of the family, it was my duty to keep you and Tesman fully informed about what he got up to last night.

HEDDA. But why, Judge Brack?

BRACK. Well, because I have a shrewd suspicion he's going to use you as some kind of screen.

HEDDA. Whatever makes you think that?

BRACK. Good God, Hedda, we're not blind, now are we? You just wait and see. I mean, you won't catch Mrs. Elvsted leaving town in a hurry.

HEDDA. But . . . assuming there is something going on between those two, there are lots of other places they can meet besides here, aren't there?

BRACK. No. Nowhere. From now on, just as before, every respectable house will be closed to Eilert Lovborg.

HEDDA. And you mean mine should be too.

BRACK. Yes. I must admit I would find it more than distressing if that man were to find sanctuary here. He'd be an intruder, a superfluous element, he would disrupt the . . . er . . .

HEDDA. The triangle?

BRACK. For me it would be as if I'd suddenly become homeless.

HEDDA. (*Looking at him and smiling.*) So, you want to be the only bull in the ring, is that your aim?

BRACK. Yes, that's my aim. And it's an aim I'll fight to achieve . . . with every means I have at my disposal.

HEDDA. I see when it comes to it you're a dangerous man.

BRACK. Do you think so?

HEDDA. Yes, I'm beginning to think so. I don't mind . . . as long as you don't have any kind of hold over me.

BRACK. (*An ambiguous laugh.*) Yes, you may be right, Hedda. If I did, who knows, I might want to take advantage of it.

HEDDA. Now, really, Judge Brack. That sounds almost like a threat.

BRACK. (*Standing up.*) Not at all. No, my point is that the defense and protection of the triangle should be voluntary.

HEDDA. I agree with you.

BRACK. Well, now I've said what I came to say, I might as well be getting back to town. Good-bye, Hedda. (*Moves toward the glass door.*)

HEDDA. (*Standing up.*) Are you going out through the garden?

BRACK. Yes, it's a short cut for me.

HEDDA. Yes, and it's also the back way, isn't it?

BRACK. Very true. I've got nothing against back ways. Sometimes they can be quite exciting.

HEDDA. You mean when there's shooting going on?

BRACK. (*In the doorway, laughing.*) Surely no one would want to shoot at their tame bull.

HEDDA. (*Also laughing.*) No, especially if it were the only one they had.

(*They nod and say good-bye, laughing. He leaves. She closes the door behind him.* HEDDA, *now quite serious, stands there for a moment, looking out. Then she goes over to the back wall and peeps through the curtains. She moves over to the writing table, takes* LOVBORG'S *parcel off the bookshelf and is about to look through the manuscript, when* BERTE'S *voice is heard loud in the hall.* HEDDA *stands and listens. Then she hurriedly pushes the parcel into a drawer, locks it and puts the key on the writing table.* LOVBORG, *still wearing his overcoat and carrying his hat, bursts through the hall door. He looks confused and upset.*)

LOVBORG. (*Turned toward the hall.*) I've told you, I must go in and I will! And that's that. (*Closes the door, turns round, sees* HEDDA, *regains his self-control immediately and bows.*)

HEDDA. (*At the writing table.*) Ah, Mr. Lovborg, you've come to collect Thea. Rather late, aren't you?

LOVBORG. You mean it's rather early to intrude on you. Please forgive me.

HEDDA. How do you know she's still here?

LOVBORG. They told me at her boarding house she'd been out all night.

HEDDA. (*Walking over to the drawing-room table.*) Did you notice anything about them when they told you that?

LOVBORG. (*Looking inquiringly at her.*) Notice anything about them?

HEDDA. I mean, did they seem to have any opinons about the matter?

LOVBORG. (*Suddenly understanding.*) Oh, yes, of course, you mean what do they think about my dragging her down with me. I'm afraid I was in no condition to notice anything. . . . I don't suppose Tesman is up yet.

HEDDA. No, I don't think so.

LOVBORG. When did he get home?

HEDDA. Very late.

LOVBORG. Did he say anything to you?

HEDDA. He told me it had all been very spirited at Judge Brack's.

LOVBORG. Is that all?

HEDDA. Yes, I think so. I was exhausted anyway.

(MRS. ELVSTED *comes in from the back room.*)

MRS. ELVSTED. (*Crossing to him.*) Oh, Lovborg. At last!

LOVBORG. Yes, at last. And too late.

MRS. ELVSTED. (*Looking at him anxiously.*) What do you mean, too late?

LOVBORG. I mean, it's all too late now. I'm finished.

MRS. ELVSTED. No, you aren't, don't say that.

LOVBORG. You'll say it as well, when I tell you what . . .

MRS. ELVSTED. I don't want you to tell me anything!

HEDDA. Perhaps you'd like to speak to her alone? I'll leave you.

LOVBORG. No, you stay as well. I want you to stay, please.

MRS. ELVSTED. I said I don't want you to tell me anything!

LOVBORG. It's not last night's adventures I want to talk to you about.

MRS. ELVSTED. What is it, then?

LOVBORG. It's that, from now on, we're going to have to split up.

MRS. ELVSTED. Split up?

HEDDA. (*Involuntarily.*) I knew it!

LOVBORG. I don't need you any more, Thea.

MRS. ELVSTED. How can you stand there and say that? You don't need me any more? I'm going to go on helping you, aren't I, as I used to? We're going to go on working together, aren't we?

LOVBORG. I've no intention of doing any more work.

MRS. ELVSTED. (*In desperation.*) Well, what do you expect me to do with my life?

LOVBORG. You must try to live the rest of your life as if you'd never met me.

MRS. ELVSTED. But how can I?

LOVBORG. You've got to try, Thea. You must go back home. . . .

MRS. ELVSTED. (*Protesting.*) Never, I couldn't. I want to be wherever you are. I'm not going to let you send me away like that. I want to stay here with you. I want to be with you when your book comes out.

HEDDA. (*Half-aloud, in suspense.*) Oh, yes, the book. . . .

LOVBORG. (*Looking at her.*) My book and Thea's. That's what it is.

MRS. ELVSTED. Yes, that's how I think of it. That's why it's my right to be with you when it comes out. I want to see you respected again and showered with honors. And happy. I want to share your happiness with you.

LOVBORG. Thea, our book is never going to come out.

HEDDA. Ah!

MRS. ELVSTED. What do you mean?

LOVBORG. It can never come out.

MRS. ELVSTED. (*A terrifying premonition.*) Lovborg, what have you done with the manuscript?

HEDDA. (*Looking at him anxiously.*) The manuscript, yes . . . ?

MRS. ELVSTED. Where is it?

LOVBORG. Thea, please don't ask me.

MRS. ELVSTED. I will ask you, I want to know. I have a right to know. Now.

LOVBORG. The manuscript . . . well, the thing is, I tore the manuscript up into a thousand pieces.

MRS. ELVSTED. (*Screaming.*) No!

HEDDA. (*Involuntarily.*) But that isn't . . . !

LOVBORG. (*Looking at her.*) You don't think it's true?

HEDDA. (*Pulling herself together.*) Well, obviously, it is. If you say so. It's just that it sounded so unlikely. . . .

LOVBORG. All the same, it's true.

MRS. ELVSTED. (*Wringing her hands.*) Oh, God. . . . Oh, God, Hedda . . . all that work, he's torn it all to pieces!

LOVBORG. I've torn my life to pieces. Why shouldn't I tear up my life's work as well . . . ?

MRS. ELVSTED. And you did that last night?

LOVBORG. Yes. Yes, I did. Into a thousand pieces. Which I then scattered into the fjord. A long way out. At least there there's cool salt water, and they can drift with the current and the wind, and after a bit they can sink. Deeper and deeper. Like me, Thea

MRS. ELVSTED. You know, Lovborg, what you've done with the book . . . it's like . . . all my life I shall think of it as if you'd killed a little child.

LOVBORG. That's right. Child murder.

MRS. ELVSTED. But how could you? It was my child as well, you know.

HEDDA. (*Almost inaudibly.*) A child . . .

MRS. ELVSTED. (*Sighing.*) That's the end of it. Yes. I'm going now, Hedda.

HEDDA. You're not going to leave town, are you?

MRS. ELVSTED. I don't know what I'm going to do. There's nothing but darkness ahead of me now. (*Exits by the hall door.*)

HEDDA. (*Stands waiting for a moment.*) Aren't you going to see her home, Mr. Lovborg?

LOVBORG. Me? Through the streets? Suppose people were to see her with me?

HEDDA. I don't know what else you did last night. Was it as irredeemable as that?

LOVBORG. Last night was only the beginning. I know that for sure. But that's not all. I also know I've got no taste for that kind of life any more either. Not all over again. She's broken my courage and my stamina.

HEDDA. (*Staring in front of her.*) That pretty little fool has had a hand in shaping a human destiny. (*Looks at him.*) Even so, I don't know how you could be so cruel to her.

LOVBORG. Don't say I was cruel.

HEDDA. To destroy something which had filled her mind for all that time. Don't you think that was cruel?

LOVBORG. I can tell you the truth, Hedda.

HEDDA. The truth?

LOVBORG. Promise me first . . . swear to me that Thea will never find out what I'm going to tell you.

HEDDA. I swear.

LOVBORG. All right. It wasn't true what I told her just now.

HEDDA. About the manuscript?

LOVBORG. I didn't tear it up. Or throw it into the fjord.

HEDDA. Then . . . if you didn't . . . where is it?

LOVBORG. I've still destroyed it. Completely.

HEDDA. I don't understand.

LOVBORG. Thea said that, for her, what I'd done was like a child murder.

HEDDA. Yes. . . .

LOVBORG. But to kill his child isn't the worst thing a father can do.

HEDDA. Isn't it?

LOVBORG. No. And I didn't want Thea to find out the worst.

HEDDA. What is the worst?

LOVBORG. Suppose that in the early hours of the morning, after a wild, drunken night out, a man came back to his child's mother and said, "Listen, these are the places I've been. I've been there and there and there. And I took our child with me. There and there and there. And I've lost the child. Completely lost him. God knows who's got hold of him. Who's got their hands on him."

HEDDA. But, I mean, when all's said and done, it was only a book.

LOVBORG. Thea's pure heart was in that book.

HEDDA. Yes, I understand.

LOVBORG. Then I expect you'll also understand that there can be no future for her and me.

HEDDA. So what are you going to do now?

LOVBORG. Nothing. Just finish it all. The sooner the better.

HEDDA. (*Moving a step nearer.*) Eilert Lovborg, listen to me. . . . Please make sure you . . . you do it beautifully.

LOVBORG. Beautifully? (*Smiles.*) With vine leaves in my hair, as you used to imagine me?

HEDDA. No, no. I don't believe in the vine leaves any more. But beautifully all the same. Just for once. Good-bye. You must go now. And never come here again.

LOVBORG. Good-bye, Mrs. Tesman. Remember me to your husband. (*Is about to leave.*)

HEDDA. No, wait. I want you to have a keepsake to remind you of me. (*Crosses to the writing table and opens the pistol case. Then she returns to* LOVBORG, *bringing one of the pistols.*)

LOVBORG. (*Looking at her.*) That? Is that the keepsake?

HEDDA. (*Nodding slowly.*) Do you recognize it? It's been aimed at you once before.

LOVBORG. You should have used it then.

HEDDA. Make sure you use it now.

LOVBORG. (*Putting the pistol in his breast pocket.*) Thank you.

HEDDA. And beautifully, Eilert Lovborg. Promise me!

LOVBORG. Good-bye, Hedda Gabler. (*Exits by the hall door.*)

(HEDDA *listens at the door for a while. Then she goes over to the writing table, takes out the parcel of manuscript, glances under the wrapping, pulls a few of the sheets halfway out and looks at them. Then she takes it over and sits in the armchair by the stove. She puts the parcel in her lap. After a while, she opens the door of the stove, then the parcel.*)

HEDDA. (*Throwing a few pages of manuscript onto the*

fire and whispering.) I'm burning your child, Thea. Curly-haired Thea. (*Throws a few more pages into the stove.*) Your child and Eilert Lovborg's child. (*Throws the rest in.*) I'm burning it, I'm burning your child.

ACT FOUR

The TESMANS' *room again. Evening. The drawing room is lit by the lamp which hangs over the table. The curtains are drawn in front of the glass door.*

HEDDA, *dressed in black, is pacing up and down in the dark room. She goes into the back room and out of sight to the* L. *A few chords are played on the piano. Then she reappears and moves back into the drawing room.* BERTE *enters from the* R. *through the back room, carrying a lighted lamp, which she puts on the table in front of the corner sofa in the living room. Her eyes are red from weeping and she has black ribbons in her cap. She exits* L., *quietly and discreetly.* HEDDA *crosses to the glass door, lifts the curtains a little and looks out into the night. A moment later,* MISS TESMAN, *dressed in mourning and wearing a hat with a veil, enters through the hall.* HEDDA *goes toward her and shakes hands with her.*

MISS TESMAN. You see me in the colors of mourning, Hedda. My poor sister has finally passed on.

HEDDA. As you can see, I've already heard the news. Tesman sent me a card.

MISS TESMAN. Yes, he promised me he would. Even so, Hedda, I felt I should announce the death myself . . . to the house of the living.

HEDDA. That was very kind of you.

MISS TESMAN. Ah, Rina should never have died now. This is no time for Hedda's house to be in mourning.

HEDDA. (*Changing the subject.*) Miss Tesman died peacefully, did she?

MISS TESMAN. Yes, it ended very gently, very calmly. And she had the inexpressible happiness of seeing George again. And being able to say good-bye to him properly. Hasn't he come back yet?

HEDDA. No. He told me not to expect him back for a bit. Er, won't you sit down?

MISS TESMAN. No, thank you, Hedda, my dear. I'd like to. But I don't have very much time. I have to lay her out and prepare her as well as I can. I want her to go to her grave looking really lovely.

HEDDA. Can I help you with anything?

MISS TESMAN. Of course not, you must put that out of your mind. We can't have Hedda Tesman turning her hand to that kind of work. Or her thoughts. Not now, not now.

HEDDA. It's not always possible to control one's thoughts.

MISS TESMAN. (*Continuing.*) Oh dear, oh dear, that's the way the world goes. At home we're sewing Rina's shroud. And soon there'll be sewing here too, if I'm not mistaken. But of a different kind, thank God.

(TESMAN *enters by the hall door.*)

HEDDA. At last, I'm glad you're here.

TESMAN. You here, Auntie Julia? With Hedda? Well, well, well.

MISS TESMAN. My dear boy, I was just about to leave. Have you managed to do all the things you promised?

TESMAN. No, I'm afraid I must have forgotten at least half of them. I'll have to pop in and see you again to-morrow morning. I'm in a complete dither today. I can't concentrate.

MISS TESMAN. But, George dear, you mustn't take it like this.

TESMAN. What do you mean?

MISS TESMAN. You must feel happiness as well as grief. You must be happy about what has happened. I am.

TESMAN. Oh, you mean Auntie Rina.

HEDDA. You're going to be very lonely now, Miss Tesman.

MISS TESMAN. At first, yes. But I'm hoping that won't last for long. I know poor Rina's room won't stay empty for very long.

TESMAN. Really? Who are you thinking of moving in then? Mm?

MISS TESMAN. Oh, well, it's a sad thing, but there's always some poor invalid needing care and attention.

HEDDA. Do you really want to take up that cross again?

MISS TESMAN. Cross? Good Lord, child, it's never seemed like a cross to me.

HEDDA. But surely a complete stranger . . .

MISS TESMAN. It doesn't take long to make friends with sick people. And I need someone to live for as well, it's very important. And thank God, an old aunt might be able to make herself useful soon, doing one or two things in this house.

HEDDA. Don't talk about us.

TESMAN. Just think what a lovely time the three of us could have together, if . . .

HEDDA. If what?

TESMAN. (*Uneasily.*) Oh, never mind. Things will sort themselves out. Let's hope so, anyway. Mm?

MISS TESMAN. Well, I expect you have one or two things to discuss. (*Smiles.*) And I think perhaps Hedda may have something to say to you, George. Good-bye. I must be getting home to Rina. (*Turns at the door.*) Good Lord, I've just had the strangest thought. Do you realize that now Rina is with me and with Jochum at the same time?

TESMAN. Yes, extraordinary, Auntie Julia, isn't it? Mm?

(*Exit* MISS TESMAN *by the hall door.*)

HEDDA. (*Following* TESMAN *with her eyes, coldly and*

searchingly.) I almost think the death has affected you more than it has her.

TESMAN. Oh, it's not only Auntie Rina. It's Eilert I'm really worried about.

HEDDA. (*Quickly.*) Have you heard anything about him?

TESMAN. I wanted to call in on him this afternoon and tell him his manuscript was being looked after.

HEDDA. And didn't you see him?

TESMAN. No. He wasn't there. But soon afterwards I met Mrs. Elvsted and she told me he'd been here early this morning.

HEDDA. That's right, just after you left.

TESMAN. And apparently he said he'd torn his manuscript to pieces. Is that true? Mm?

HEDDA. So he maintained, yes.

TESMAN. Good God, he must have been completely out of his mind. I suppose you didn't dare give it back to him then, Hedda.

HEDDA. I didn't give it back to him, no.

TESMAN. But obviously you told him we had it.

HEDDA. No. (*Quickly.*) Did you tell Mrs. Elvsted?

TESMAN. No, I thought I'd better not. But you ought to have told him. He must be very desperate about it, suppose he were to go and do something rash. Let's have the manuscript, Hedda. I'd better run round with it straightaway. Where've you put it?

HEDDA. (*Leaning on the armchair, cold and motionless.*) I haven't got it.

TESMAN. You haven't got it? What do you mean, you haven't got it?

HEDDA. I burnt it. The whole thing.

TESMAN. (*Leaping up, horrified.*) Burnt it? Burnt Eilert's manuscript?

HEDDA. Don't shout like that. The maid might hear you.

TESMAN. Burnt it? My God, no, you can't have done, it's impossible.

HEDDA. It may be, nevertheless that's what happened.

TESMAN. Do you realize what you've done, Hedda? It's illegal disposal of lost property. It's extraordinary. You ask Judge Brack, he'll tell you a few things.

HEDDA. I don't think it would be a very good idea to discuss it with Judge Brack . . . or, indeed, anyone.

TESMAN. But how could you do such a monstrous thing? How could you even think of it? What came over you? Mm? Answer me, mm?

HEDDA. (*Suppressing an almost-imperceptible smile.*) I did it for your sake, George.

TESMAN. For my sake?

HEDDA. When you came home this morning and told me he'd read to you . . .

TESMAN. Yes, yes, go on.

HEDDA. You said you'd envied him because of his book.

TESMAN. Yes, but I mean, I didn't mean it quite so literally.

HEDDA. Even so, I couldn't bear the thought that anyone should overshadow you.

TESMAN. (*An outburst of mixed doubt and joy.*) Hedda . . . is that true? But I mean . . . but I mean . . . you've never shown your love like this before. It's extraordinary.

HEDDA. Yes, well, perhaps it's the best time for you to find out about it . . . just when . . . (*Breaks off abruptly.*) No, you'd better go and ask Aunt Julia. She'll tell you quick enough.

TESMAN. I think I understand you, Hedda, I think I do. (*Claps his hands.*) Is it true, is it, mm?

HEDDA. Don't shout like that. The maid'll hear you.

TESMAN. (*Laughing, overjoyed.*) The maid! I like that, Hedda, you are priceless! The maid . . . Berte you mean, you mean Berte! I'll go and tell Berte myself.

HEDDA. (*Clenching her fists in desperation.*) It's killing me, all this, it's killing me.

TESMAN. What is, Hedda? Mm?

HEDDA. (*Cold, controlled.*) It's all so . . . ridiculous . . . George.

TESMAN. Ridiculous? What's ridiculous about my being so pleased and happy? Perhaps . . . perhaps I'd better not say anything to Berte after all.

HEDDA. Why not?

TESMAN. Well, not just yet, anyway. But I must certainly tell Auntie Julia. I must tell her you've started calling me George, as well. What about that, Auntie Julia will be so pleased, she'll be so pleased.

HEDDA. When you tell her I burnt Eilert Lovborg's manuscript, for your sake?

TESMAN. Oh, yes, that, well, of course, no one must know about the manuscript. But your love for me, Hedda, I really must tell Auntie Julia about that. I wonder if this kind of thing is usual with newlyweds, what do you think? Mm?

HEDDA. You'd better ask Auntie Julia about that as well.

TESMAN. Yes, I will, I will, if I get the opportunity. (*Seems uneasy and reflective again.*) As for the . . . er . . . the manuscript . . . My God, it's terrible to think what's going to happen to Eilert now.

(MRS. ELVSTED, *dressed as she was at her first appearance, wearing her hat and coat, enters by the hall door.*)

MRS. ELVSTED. (*Acknowledging them hastily and speaking agitatedly.*) Oh, Hedda, don't be angry with me for coming back.

HEDDA. What's the matter with you, Thea?

TESMAN. Is it something about Eilert Lovborg? Mm?

MRS. ELVSTED. Yes, I'm terribly afraid he's had some accident.

HEDDA. (*Catching hold of her arm.*) Do you think so?

TESMAN. Yes, but, I mean, what makes you think that, Mrs. Elvsted?

MRS. ELVSTED. I heard them talking about him at my hotel . . . just as I came in. The most incredible rumors about him have been going around all day.

TESMAN. Yes, I've been hearing them as well, can you imagine? And I know he went straight home to bed last night, I'm a witness. It's extraordinary.

HEDDA. What were they saying at the hotel?

MRS. ELVSTED. I found nothing out. Either because they didn't know anything very definite, or because . . . They stopped talking as soon as they saw me. And I didn't dare ask.

TESMAN. (*Moving around uneasily.*) Well, let's hope you misunderstood them, Mrs. Elvsted.

MRS. ELVSTED. No, I'm sure it was him they were talking about. And I heard them say something about the hospital and . . .

TESMAN. The hospital?

HEDDA. No, that's impossible.

MRS. ELVSTED. I got desperately frightened. So I went up to his boarding house and asked them about him.

HEDDA. How could you bring yourself to do that?

MRS. ELVSTED. What else could I have done? I felt I couldn't stand the uncertainty any longer.

TESMAN. And I suppose you didn't find him there either? Mm?

MRS. ELVSTED. No. And the people there knew nothing about him. They said he hadn't been back there since yesterday afternoon.

TESMAN. Yesterday afternoon? But that's impossible.

MRS. ELVSTED. So I'm sure something awful must have happened to him.

TESMAN. Hedda, perhaps I should go into town and inquire around a bit . . . ?

HEDDA. No, no, there's no need for you to get mixed up in this.

(JUDGE BRACK, *carrying his hat, comes in through the*

hall door, shown in by BERTE. *He looks very serious and bows silently.*)

TESMAN. Ah, Judge, it's you, is it? Mm?

BRACK. Yes, I felt I had to come and see you this evening.

TESMAN. I can see by your face you've heard the news from Auntie Julia.

BRACK. I've heard about that as well, yes.

TESMAN. Tragic, isn't it? Mm?

BRACK. Well, my dear Tesman, it depends how you look at it.

TESMAN. (*Looking at him uncertainly.*) Is there something else as well?

BRACK. Yes. There is.

HEDDA. (*Tensely.*) Something tragic, Judge Brack?

BRACK. It depends how you look at it, Mrs. Tesman.

MRS. ELVSTED. (*An involuntary outburst.*) It's something to do with Eilert Lovborg!

BRACK. (*Glancing at her.*) Whatever makes you think that, Mrs. Elvsted? Perhaps you've heard about it already . . . ?

MRS. ELVSTED. (*Confused.*) No, I haven't, no, it's just . . .

TESMAN. For goodness' sake, tell us!

BRACK. (*Shrugging his shoulders.*) Well, I'm sorry to say, Eilert Lovborg has been taken to hospital. He's dying.

MRS. ELVSTED. (*Screaming.*) Oh, God, oh, my God . . . !

TESMAN. Taken to hospital? Dying?

HEDDA. (*Involuntarily.*) So soon . . .

MRS. ELVSTED. (*Moaning.*) And we separated without making it up, Hedda!

HEDDA. (*Whispering.*) Thea, really, dear!

MRS. ELVSTED. (*Taking no notice.*) I must go to him! I must see him alive!

BRACK. It's no use, Mrs. Elvsted. No one's allowed to see him.

MRS. ELVSTED. Can't you just tell me what's happened to him? How did it happen?

TESMAN. He hasn't . . . erm . . . er, has he? Mm?

HEDDA. Yes, I'm sure he has.

TESMAN. Hedda, how could you . . . ?

BRACK. (*Who has been watching her all the time.*) I'm afraid you've guessed right, Mrs. Tesman.

MRS. ELVSTED. How terrible!

TESMAN. You mean he has? Extraordinary.

HEDDA. Shot himself.

BRACK. Right again, Mrs. Tesman.

MRS. ELVSTED. (*Trying to control herself.*) When did it happen, Judge?

BRACK. This afternoon. Between three and four.

TESMAN. Oh, my God, where was he when he did it? Mm?

BRACK. (*Slightly thrown.*) Where? He . . . er . . . I suppose at his lodgings.

MRS. ELVSTED. No, he can't have been. I was there between six and seven.

BRACK. Well, somewhere else then. I'm not sure. I only know he was found. . . . He'd shot himself in the chest.

MRS. ELVSTED. It's horrible to think of him dying like that!

HEDDA. (*To* BRACK.) In the chest, did you say?

BRACK. I did, yes.

HEDDA. Not in the temple?

BRACK. In the chest, Mrs. Tesman.

HEDDA. Yes, well . . . that will do.

BRACK. What do you mean?

HEDDA. (*Evasively.*) Oh, nothing, nothing.

TESMAN. And you say the wound is dangerous, is it? Mm?

BRACK. Yes, absolutely fatal. It's probably all over already.

MRS. ELVSTED. It is, I know it is! It's all over. All over. Oh, Hedda!

TESMAN. But tell me . . . how did you find out all this?

BRACK. (*Shortly.*) From someone in the police. A man I was talking to.

HEDDA. (*Penetratingly.*) At last, an achievement!

TESMAN. (*Shocked.*) Good heavens, Hedda, what do you mean?

HEDDA. I mean, there's something beautiful about it.

BRACK. Mrs. Tesman . . .

TESMAN. What do you mean, beautiful? Extraordinary thing to say.

MRS. ELVSTED. Oh, Hedda, how can you talk about beauty after what's happened?

HEDDA. Eilert Lovborg has had a reckoning with himself. He has had the courage to do what . . . what was right.

MRS. ELVSTED. You mustn't think it happened like that, it didn't. What he did was an act of despair.

TESMAN. An act of total despair, that's what it was.

HEDDA. No, it wasn't. I'm sure it wasn't.

MRS. ELVSTED. It was! Despair. Like when he tore up our book.

BRACK. (*Puzzled.*) Book? Do you mean his manuscript? Did he tear that up?

MRS. ELVSTED. Yes, last night.

TESMAN. (*Whispering softly.*) Oh, Hedda, we're never going to get away with this.

BRACK. Really, that's very curious.

TESMAN. (*Crossing the room.*) It's terrible to think of Eilert passing on like this. Without leaving behind the thing that would have immortalized his name. . . .

MRS. ELVSTED. If only it could be pieced together again . . .

TESMAN. Yes, if only it could! I don't know what I wouldn't give to . . .

MRS. ELVSTED. Perhaps it could, Mr. Tesman.

TESMAN. What do you mean?

MRS. ELVSTED. (*Searching in her handbag.*) Look. I've kept all these loose scraps of paper he used to have with him when he dictated.

HEDDA. (*Moving a step nearer.*) Ah!

TESMAN. You kept them, did you, Mrs. Elvsted? Mm?

MRS. ELVSTED. Yes, here they are. I brought them with me when I came. And they've been lying in my bag ever since. . . .

TESMAN. Let's have a look!

MRS. ELVSTED. (*Passing him a handful of scraps of paper.*) But they're not in any order. They're completely mixed up.

TESMAN. Can you imagine, if we could work it out anyway? Perhaps if we helped each other . . .

MRS. ELVSTED. Oh, yes, let's at least try it . . .

TESMAN. It will work. It's got to work! I'll devote my life to it.

HEDDA. Your life, George?

TESMAN. Yes, well, I mean, all the time I can spare. I'll put aside my own research for a while. Do you understand me, Hedda? Mm? I owe it to Eilert's memory.

HEDDA. Possibly.

TESMAN. Well, Mrs. Elvsted, let's pull ourselves together, shall we? I mean, Good Lord, there's no sense in brooding about what's already happened, is there? Mm? We must do our best to find sufficient peace of mind to . . .

MRS. ELVSTED. Yes, Mrs. Tesman, I'll try as hard as I can.

TESMAN. Well, come on then. Let's have a look at these notes right away. Where shall we sit? Here? No, let's go in the back room. Would you excuse me, Judge? Come along, Mrs. Elvsted.

MRS. ELVSTED. Oh, God, if only it were possible.

(TESMAN *and* MRS. ELVSTED *go into the back room. She takes off her hat and overcoat. They sit at the table, under the hanging lamp, and are soon engrossed in searching eagerly through the papers.* HEDDA *crosses to the stove and sits in the armchair. A moment later* BRACK *joins her.*)

HEDDA. (*Half-aloud.*) Oh, Judge, there's such a sense of release in what Eilert Lovborg's done.

BRACK. Release? Well, it was certainly a release for him. . . .

HEDDA. I meant for me. It's a release to know that in spite of everything a premeditated act of courage is still possible. Something with at least some spark of instinctive beauty.

BRACK. (*Smiling.*) Well, Hedda . . .

HEDDA. Oh, I know what you're going to say. You're a kind of academic, too, aren't you, like . . . aren't you?

BRACK. (*Watching her closely.*) Eilert Lovborg meant more to you than you perhaps want to admit, even to yourself. Or am I quite mistaken?

HEDDA. I'm not going to answer questions like that. All I know is that Eilert Lovborg had the courage to live his life the way he wanted to live it. To its final great and beautiful achievement. When he had the strength and willpower to walk out on life . . . early.

BRACK. It grieves me, Hedda . . . but I'm afraid I'm going to have to shatter an agreeable illusion.

HEDDA. Illusion?

BRACK. Which couldn't have lasted long in any case.

HEDDA. What do you mean?

BRACK. His shooting himself. It wasn't . . . premeditated.

HEDDA. Wasn't premeditated?

BRACK. No. What I said about Eilert wasn't entirely accurate.

HEDDA. (*In suspense.*) Have you kept something back? What?

BRACK. For the sake of poor Mrs. Elvsted, I felt it necessary to employ a few little euphemisms.

HEDDA. Go on.

BRACK. Well, in the first place, he's already dead.

HEDDA. At the hospital?

BRACK. Yes. He died without regaining consciousness.

HEDDA. What else?

BRACK. It . . . er . . . didn't happen in his room.

HEDDA. Well, I don't see that that matters very much.

BRACK. I think it may do. You see, I might as well tell you, Eilert Lovborg was found shot in . . . Miss Diana's . . . room.

HEDDA. (*Starting to jump up, then sinking back.*) But that's impossible. He can't have been round there again today.

BRACK. He went round there this afternoon. He went to demand something he said they'd taken from him. Told some incomprehensible story about a lost child. . . .

HEDDA. Oh, that's it. . . .

BRACK. I thought he might have been talking about his manuscript. But now I'm told he destroyed that himself. Perhaps he meant his notebook.

HEDDA. Yes, he must have done. So . . . so he was found there?

BRACK. Yes. With an empty pistol in his inside pocket. And a fatal wound.

HEDDA. In the chest. . . .

BRACK. No . . . somewhat lower.

HEDDA. (*Looks up at him with an expression of disgust.*) It's like some curse, everything I touch turns into something ludicrous and disgusting.

BRACK. There's another thing, Hedda. Another unpleasant aspect of the case.

HEDDA. What?

BRACK. The pistol he had with him . . .

HEDDA. (*Breathlessly.*) What about it?

BRACK. Must have been stolen.

HEDDA. (*Jumping up.*) Stolen? That's not true! It wasn't!

BRACK. It's the only possible explanation. He must have stolen it. . . . Ssh!

(TESMAN *and* MRS. ELVSTED *have risen from the table in the back room and move into the drawing room.*)

TESMAN. (*Hands full of papers.*) Can you imagine, Hedda, it's almost impossible for me to see anything under that lamp.

HEDDA. Yes, I can imagine.

TESMAN. Might we be allowed to sit at your writing table for a bit? Mm?

HEDDA. Yes, all right. (*Quickly.*) No, wait a minute! Let me clear it first.

TESMAN. There's no need to, Hedda. There's plenty of room.

HEDDA. I said let me clear it. I'll just put these things on the piano for the time being. There we are. (*She has pulled something out from under the bookshelf, invisible under sheet music, piles some more sheet music on top of it and moves to the* L., *carrying the whole lot into the back room.* TESMAN *puts his papers on the writing-table and moves the lamp over from the corner table. He and* MRS. ELVSTED *sit down and start working again.* HEDDA *returns.* HEDDA, *behind* MRS. ELVSTED'S *chair, running her fingers through her hair.*) Dear Thea . . . how's it going with Eilert Lovborg's memorial?

MRS. ELVSTED. (*Looking at her, somewhat dispirited.*) It's going to be terribly difficult sorting it all out.

TESMAN. It's got to work. There's no alternative. Anyway, sorting out, collating other people's papers is exactly what I'm best at.

(HEDDA *crosses the room and sits on one of the stools.* BRACK *stands over her, leaning against the armchair.*)

HEDDA. (*Whispering.*) What were you saying about the pistol?

BRACK. (*Quietly.*) That he must have stolen it.
HEDDA. Why should he have stolen it?
BRACK. It's the only possible explanation, Hedda.
HEDDA. Is it?
BRACK. (*Glancing at her.*) Eilert Lovborg was here this morning, wasn't he?
HEDDA. Yes.
BRACK. Were you alone with him?
HEDDA. Yes, for a bit.
BRACK. You didn't leave the room while he was here?
HEDDA. No.
BRACK. Are you sure? Not even for a minute?
HEDDA. Well, perhaps just for a minute, when I went out to the hall.
BRACK. And where was your pistol-case this morning?
HEDDA. Locked in the . . .
BRACK. Really, Hedda?
HEDDA. No, over there on the writing table.
BRACK. And have you checked to see if both pistols are still there?
HEDDA. No.
BRACK. You needn't bother. I saw the pistol Lovborg had on him. I recognized it immediately as one I'd seen yesterday. And on previous occasions.
HEDDA. Have you got it?
BRACK. No, the police have got it.
HEDDA. What will the police do with it?
BRACK. Try to track down its owner.
HEDDA. Do you think they'll succeed?
BRACK. (*Bending over her and whispering.*) No, Hedda Gabler, as long as I don't say anything.
HEDDA. (*Looking up at him, frightened.*) And what if you do say something?
BRACK. (*Shrugging his shoulders.*) You could always tell them the pistol was stolen.
HEDDA. (*Firmly.*) I'd rather die.
BRACK. (*Smiling.*) People say things like that. But they never do them.

HEDDA. (*Without answering.*) And suppose the pistol wasn't stolen? And they find the owner? What then?

BRACK. Then, Hedda, I expect there would be a scandal.

HEDDA. A scandal?

BRACK. Yes, the kind of scandal you're so terribly afraid of. You'd have to go to court, of course. You and Miss Diana. She'll have to explain how it happened. Whether it was an accident or murder. Was he trying to take the pistol out of his pocket to threaten her, when it suddenly went off? Or did she wrench the pistol out of his hand, shoot him and put it back in his pocket? That would be quite like her. She's quite a beefy young lady, Miss Diana.

HEDDA. But all that vile business has got nothing to do with me.

BRACK. No. You'll just have to answer one question: Why did you give Eilert Lovborg the pistol? And when it comes out that you did give it to him, what inevitable conclusions do you suppose people will jump to?

HEDDA. (*Her head sinking.*) I see. I hadn't thought of that.

BRACK. Fortunately, of course, as long as I keep quiet about it, there's no danger.

HEDDA. (*Looking up at him.*) So, I'm in your power, am I, Judge? From now on you do have a hold over me.

BRACK. (*Whispering softly.*) Dearest Hedda . . . believe me . . . I shan't take advantage of my position.

HEDDA. I'll still be in your power. Dependent on your demands and whims. A slave. I'll be a slave. (*Gets up quickly.*) No, I can't bear the thought of it! I can't!

BRACK. (*Looking at her, half-scornfully.*) As a rule, one comes to accept the inevitable.

HEDDA. (*Returning his gaze.*) Possibly. (*Crosses to the writing table.* HEDDA, *suppressing an involuntary smile and imitating* TESMAN'S *intonation.*) Well? How are you getting on, George? Mm?

TESMAN. God knows. There's months of work here, months, at least.

HEDDA. (*As before.*) Extraordinary. (*Runs her fingers through* MRS. ELVSTED'S *hair.*) Don't you find it strange, Thea? Sitting here with Tesman, as you used to sit with Eilert Lovborg?

MRS. ELVSTED. If only I could inspire your husband in the same way.

HEDDA. I'm sure you will. Given time.

TESMAN. It's a funny thing, Hedda, but I really think something of the sort is beginning to happen. Now, go and sit down and talk to the Judge again.

HEDDA. Is there nothing I can do to make myself useful?

TESMAN. No, not a thing. (*Turns his head.*) Can I leave Hedda for you to look after from now on, Judge?

BRACK. (*Glancing at* HEDDA.) Of course, with the greatest of pleasure.

HEDDA. Thank you. I'm tired this evening. I think I'll go and lie down on the sofa in there for a bit.

TESMAN. Yes, why don't you, dear? Mm?

(HEDDA *goes into the back room, drawing the curtains behind her. A brief pause. Suddenly she is heard playing a wild dance tune on the piano.*)

MRS. ELVSTED. (*Jumping up from her chair.*) Ah . . . what's that?

TESMAN. (*Running over to the doorway.*) Please, Hedda dear, I don't think dance music is very appropriate this evening. What about Auntie Rina? And Eilert?

HEDDA. (*Putting her head out between the curtains.*) And Auntie Julia. And all the rest of them. . . . From now on I'm not going to make any more noise. (*She closes the curtain again.*)

TESMAN. (*At the writing table.*) It's not good for her, you know, seeing us doing this melancholy work. I tell you what, Mrs. Elvsted, why don't you move in with my

Auntie Julia? Then I could come up in the evenings. And we could sit and work there, couldn't we? Mm?

MRS. ELVSTED. Well, that might be an idea. . . .

HEDDA. (*From the back room.*) I can hear what you're saying, Tesman. How do you suppose I'm going to while away my evenings here?

TESMAN. (*Looking through the papers.*) I'm sure Judge Brack will be kind enough to come over and see you, even if I'm not here.

BRACK. (*Calling out happily from the armchair.*) Every evening, Mrs. Tesman, without fail. I'm sure the two of us will have a really enjoyable time together.

HEDDA. (*Loud and clear.*) That's what you're hoping for, isn't it, Judge? Now you're the only bull in the ring . . .

(*A shot rings out from within.* TESMAN, MRS. ELVSTED *and* BRACK *leap to their feet.*)

TESMAN. I suppose she's playing with those pistols again. (*Throws back the curtains and hurries in, followed by* MRS. ELVSTED. HEDDA *is lying dead, stretched out on the sofa. Confusion and cries.* BERTE *comes rushing in from the* R. TESMAN, *shouting at* BRACK.) She's shot herself! She's shot herself in the head! Extraordinary!

BRACK. (*Half-helpless in the armchair.*) What do you mean, my God, people don't do things like that!

PROPERTY PLOT

ACT ONE—PRESET:

PIANO:
Music on top
2 flower vases D. end

U. R. TABLE:
2 cigars
Dried flowers
Matches
Ashtray

U. L. TABLE:
1 flower vase

L. TABLE
Gun case (empty)
Cigarette case
2 cigarettes in case
Matches
Ashtray

BOOKCASE:
Photo album (No. 2 shelf in corner)

Off Stage D. R.:
Books
Trunk
Briefcase with documents
Flower basket and card
Footstool
Fire extinguisher

Off Stage U. R. PROP TABLE:
Lamp
2 manuscripts (1 before, 1 after, different wrappings)
Letter from Aunt Julia
Letter from Tesman to Lovborg
Parasol
Bag (with 2 slippers wrapped up inside)
1 cigar

Tray with:
Cookies and 4 glasses
Punch bowl and ladle
10 or 12 books—uncut pages
Off Stage L.:
2 guns:
1 with 1 shot for Hedda
1 with 2 shots for ASM

GENERAL:
2 dust covers:
1 on large chair
1 on sofa
3 dining-room table chairs (2 U., 1 L.)
1 medium round table U. R.
1 small round table D. of piano
1 writing desk L.
1 sofa L. C.
1 large chair R. C.
1 piano U. L.
1 bookcase with brass gewgaw top shelf
1 stove on tile foot pate
1 wood bucket and wood
1 picture General Gabler U. C. wall
1 sabre U. C. wall

PERSONAL PROPS—MRS. ELVSTED:
Card with Lovborg address on it
1 bundle notes for manuscript

PERSONAL PROPS—BRACK:
Cane
Between Acts One and Two (Ibsen):
Give Hedda gun with 1 shot L.
ASM fire 2 shots on cue L.
Between Acts Two and Three (Ibsen) Our Int.
RESET:
Chair to U. L. wall
Lamp to U. R. table
Photo album to bookcase
Large chair—face stove
Empty gun in case U. L.
Footstool front of chair
Add documents to shelves of bookcase

STRIKE:
- Punch bowl and ladle
- Glasses
- Tray
- Cookies
- Book from U. R. table

Between Acts Three and Four (Ibsen):
- Get gun from Lovborg (reload)
- Check fire

End Act Four (Ibsen)
- Fire gun

PERISHABLES—CONSUMABLES:
- Punch (tea and lemon slices)
- Cigars
- Cigarettes—Bravos for (Hedda)
- Cookies

COSTUME PLOT

HEDDA:

Act One:

Gray dress, gray morning coat, blouse, corset, stockings, gray boots, petticoat.

Act Two:

Gray jacket.

Act Three:

Red and black shawl.

Act Four:

Black skirt, black bodice, black blouse, black petticoat, black boots.

TESMAN:

Act One:

Coat, vest, trousers, socks, black shoes, suspenders, watch chain, collar, collar stud, ascot, shirt, undershirt.

Act Two:

Dress suit, ascot, coat, vest, trousers, suspenders.

Act Three:

No Change.

Act Four:

No Change.

MRS. ELVSTED:

Acts One and Two:

Skirt, blouse, corset, jacket, bodice, boots, stockings, pocketbook.

Act Three:

Remove bodice.

Act Four:

Same.

MISS TESMAN:

Act One:

Skirt, blouse, bodice, boots, corset, hat, large pocketbook, petticoats, stockings.
No Change.

LOVBORG:

Act Two:

Suit, vest, shoes, socks, undershirt, shirt, suspenders, collar, tie.

Act Three:

Same as Act 2, jacket ripped.

MAID:

Dress, apron, boots, corset, petticoat.

BRACK:

Suit, vest, shirt, collar, ascot, watch chain, socks, undershirt, suspenders.

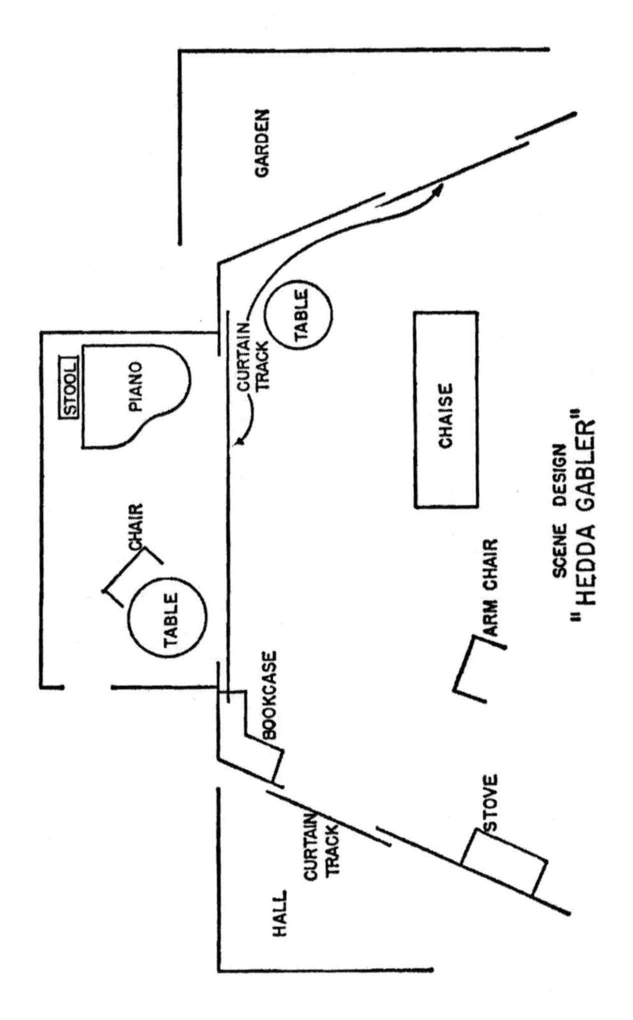
GARDEN
STOOL
PIANO
CURTAIN TRACK
TABLE
CHAISE
CHAIR
TABLE
SCENE DESIGN
"HEDDA GABLER"
ARM CHAIR
BOOKCASE
STOVE
CURTAIN TRACK
HALL

OTHER TITLES AVAILABLE FROM SAMUEL FRENCH

CAPTIVE

Jan Buttram

Comedy / 2m, 1f / Interior

A hilarious take on a father/daughter relationship, this off beat comedy combines foreign intrigue with down home philosophy. Sally Pound flees a bad marriage in New York and arrives at her parent's home in Texas hoping to borrow money from her brother to pay a debt to gangsters incurred by her husband. Her elderly parents are supposed to be vacationing in Israel, but she is greeted with a shotgun aimed by her irascible father who has been left home because of a minor car accident and is not at all happy to see her. When a news report indicates that Sally's mother may have been taken captive in the Middle East, Sally's hard-nosed brother insists that she keep father home until they receive definite word, and only then will he loan Sally the money. Sally fails to keep father in the dark, and he plans a rescue while she finds she is increasingly unable to skirt the painful truths of her life. The ornery father and his loveable but slightly-dysfunctional daughter come to a meeting of hearts and minds and solve both their problems.